THE

LITERARY JOURNAL

IN AMERICA

TO 1900

AMERICAN LITERATURE, ENGLISH LITERATURE, AND WORLD LITERATURES IN ENGLISH: AN INFORMATION GUIDE SERIES

Series Editor: Theodore Grieder, Curator, Division of Special Collections, Fales Library, New York University, New York, New York

Associate Editor: Duane DeVries, Assistant Professor, Polytechnic Institute of New York, Brooklyn, New York

Other books on American literature in this series:

THE LITERARY JOURNAL IN AMERICA, 1900-1950—*Edited by Edward E. Chielens***

AMERICAN FICTION TO 1900—*Edited by David K. Kirby**

AMERICAN FICTION, 1900-1950—*Edited by James Woodress*

AFRO-AMERICAN FICTION—*Edited by Robert A. Corrigan***

AMERICAN DRAMA TO 1900—*Edited by Walter J. Meserve***

AMERICAN DRAMA, 1900-1950—*Edited by Paul Hurley***

AMERICAN PROSE AND CRITICISM TO 1820—*Edited by Donald Yannella and John Roch***

AMERICAN PROSE AND CRITICISM, 1820-1900—*Edited by Elinore H. Partridge***

AMERICAN POETRY TO 1900—*Edited by Bernice Slote***

AMERICAN POETRY, 1900-1950—*Edited by William White and Artem Lozynsky***

* in press
** in preparation

The above series is part of the
GALE INFORMATION GUIDE LIBRARY

The Library consists of a number of separate series of guides covering major areas in the social sciences, humanities, and current affairs.

General Editor: Paul Wasserman, Professor and former Dean, School of Library and Information Services, University of Maryland

THE

LITERARY JOURNAL

IN AMERICA

TO 1900

A GUIDE TO INFORMATION SOURCES

*Volume 3 in the American Literature, English
Literature, and World Literatures in English
Information Guide Series*

Edward E. Chielens

Assistant Professor of English, Detroit College of Business

Gale Research Company
Book Tower, Detroit, Michigan 48226

**Library of Congress
Cataloging in Publication Data**

Chielens, Edward E
  The literary journal in America to 1900.

  (American literature, English literature, and world
literatures in English ; v. 3) (Gale information guide
library)
    1. American periodicals--History--Bibliography.
2. American literature--Periodicals--Bibliography.
I. Title.
Z6951.C57   016.81'05   74-11533
ISBN 0-8103-1239-5

CONTENTS

VITA

Edward E. Chielens is currently an assistant professor of English at the Detroit College of Business. He received his B.A. and Ph.D. from Wayne State University and his M.A. from the University of Michigan.

Chielens has contributed to the journal CRITICISM.

Chapter 1

INTRODUCTION

Chapter 1

INTRODUCTION

Early Periodicals: High Rates of Founding and Failure

The most striking characteristic revealed in this bibliography and not immediately apparent to the student of nineteenth-century American literature is the vast number of literary periodicals founded throughout the country in the most unlikely places and at the most unlikely times, almost all of which have been long forgotten. This publishing impulse appears in Lexington, Kentucky, as early as 1803 with the founding of THE MEDLEY, and in Hastings, Minnesota, in 1859 with THE FRONTIER MONTHLY, only one year after that state entered the union.[1] And these were not isolated cases, as this comment by Herbert Fleming about Chicago's literary periodicals shows: "All told, at least 306 magazines and journals, whose generic mark is an appeal chiefly to the aesthetic or artistic sense, have sprung up in Chicago...."[2] This bibliography can of course include studies of, or even mention, only a small fraction of these publications, and in fact for many of them no extant files or even individual copies have been found at all.

And yet accompanying this impulse to found literary periodicals is a second striking phenomenon--the universally high rate of failure to sustain publication. For instance, according to Frank Luther Mott, whose study of American periodicals is the most exhaustive ever written, four to five thousand such publications appeared during the years 1825 to 1850, and the average life span was a mere two years.[3] Many periodicals in fact failed to survive past their first numbers, the best-known case being Elizabeth Peabody's AESTHETIC PAPERS. Even some of the periodicals best remembered today were failures or considered to be so by their editors and publishers. THE MONTHLY ANTHOLOGY AND BOSTON REVIEW, published from 1805 to 1811, pioneered the way for the founding of THE NORTH AMERICAN REVIEW in 1815, and is considered by Lewis P. Simpson to have played an important role in the rise of Boston as a literary center.[4] But THE MONTHLY ANTHOLOGY lasted only six years, and although generally confident and cheerful about their enterprise, the editors in their final address in the June 1811 issue revealed some of their problems:

> At the commencement of the year we hinted at some of the inconveniences which arise from the manner in which the Anthology has been conducted and suggested our hopes that we should be relieved

> from them by giving the principle care of the publication to a
> permanent editor. In this we have been disappointed, from the
> inadequacy of the receipts of the Anthology to repay the labour
> of any gentleman to whom we should be willing to confide it.
> Our auxiliaries also, at no time numerous though always valuable,
> have lately been diminished....It may be, however, that at some
> future day we shall attempt to revive it, and possibly in a new
> form and under brighter auspices.[5]

Another important periodical which failed to prosper was James Russell Lowell's
1843 enterprise, THE PIONEER. In its three issues were published such well-
known works as Nathaniel Hawthorne's "The Birthmark" and "The Hall of Fan-
tasy," Edgar Allan Poe's "The Tell-Tale Heart," and poetry by John Greenleaf
Whittier. This quality did not save THE PIONEER from a sudden death caused
by financial troubles between editors Lowell and Robert Carter and their printers. Even before that, Lowell had tired of handling the business details and
argued with Carter about publishing policies. Perhaps the best-known literary
journalistic failure was the Transcendental DIAL, the lack of financial success
and even at times the quality of which disappointed its two major editors, Margaret Fuller and Ralph Waldo Emerson. Fuller often had to write filler material
for the journal, and when in 1842 she became too tired and discouraged, Emerson reluctantly took over as editor, only to find himself paying a $300 debt
when THE DIAL failed two years later.[6] Writing in the Chicago DIAL in 1899,
J.F.A. Pyre looked back to the earlier journal and commented on its "appeal
of brilliant promise, early death, and pathetic unfulfillments."[7] He could have
said the same of many nineteenth-century literary journals.

Major Literary Figures and the Periodicals

The "appeal of brilliant promise" was especially strong in many of these journals,
no matter what their fates were. A number of major writers worked as editors
of, or were otherwise deeply involved with, these publications at different times
in their careers. The seriousness with which they took their duties often showed
a commitment to influence the literary history of their country or to promote a
specific literary ideal or movement. The stated purpose of Lowell's and Carter's
PIONEER provides an example of this seriousness:

> The object of the subscribers, in establishing the PIONEER, is to
> furnish the intelligent and reflecting portion of the Reading Public
> with a rational substitute for the enormous quantity of thrice-diluted
> trash, in the shape of namby-pamby love tales and sketches, which
> is monthly poured out of them by many of our popular Magazines,
> --and to offer, instead thereof, a healthy and manly Periodical
> Literature, whose perusal will not necessarily involve a loss of time
> and a deterioration of every moral and intellectual faculty.[8]

Not even Lowell viewed the profession more seriously, however, than Edgar Allan Poe, whose work as editor and journalistic critic is still a subject of controversy. Poe edited THE SOUTHERN LITERARY MESSENGER, BURTON'S GEN-
TLEMAN'S MAGAZINE, GRAHAM'S MAGAZINE, and THE BROADWAY JOUR-
NAL, and was involved in such work as much or more than any other figure

mentioned in this bibliography. But he remained dissatisfied because he had to work for publishers whose aims were not compatible with his own serious views of the role of the literary journal in shaping and criticizing literature. He longed for his own periodical, which he planned to name first the PENN and then the STYLUS, and he even went so far as to gather material for it and write a tentative prospectus. His plans reveal the vital role he envisioned for the publication:

> It shall be the first and chief purpose of the Magazine now pro-
> posed to become known as one where may be found at all times,
> and upon all subjects, an honest and a fearless opinion. It shall
> be a leading object to assert in precept, and to maintain in prac-
> tice the rights, while in effect it demonstrates the advantages, of
> an absolutely independent criticism--a criticism self-sustained;
> guiding itself only by the purest rules of Art, analyzing and urging
> these rules as it applies them; holding itself aloof from all personal
> bias; acknowledging no fear save that of outraging the right, yield-
> ing no point either to the vanity of the author, or to the assump-
> tions of antique prejudice, or to the involute and anonymous cant
> of the Quarterlies, or to the arrogance of those organized cliques
> which, hanging light nightmares upon American literature, manu-
> facture, at the nod of our principal booksellers, a pseudo-public-
> opinion by wholesale.[9]

Poe's projected journal never appeared, but even as an unrealized dream it ex-
emplifies two aspects of many nineteenth-century literary journals--the serious
intent of those who undertook such work, including major writers, and the fee-
bleness of the result.

However, to portray the involvement of major figures in the field of literary
journalism as inevitably unsatisfactory, either financially or critically, would be
a distortion. Poe was discontented with the policies of the journals on which
he worked, Emerson was not completely satisfied with THE DIAL's contents, and
these two men along with Lowell had financial difficulties with their periodicals.
But other writers, Bret Harte and William Dean Howells the best known among
them, found editing a much more rewarding experience. Both in fact gained
national reputations through their work with periodicals.

Harte became an editor in July 1868 when Anton Roman, a San Francisco book-
seller, founded THE OVERLAND MONTHLY, and when Harte left the publication two-and-a-half years later he had become nationally known. The 32-year-
old editor had by 1868 published one book of poetry and one of prose, but had
no literary reputation to speak of. This situation was, however, to change, for
when no stories depicting California life were submitted for the first number of
the OVERLAND, Harte decided to supply his own "The Luck of Roaring Camp"
for the second. The story ran into trouble when the printer confronted Roman
with the proof sheets, as Harte himself said, "with the emphatic declaration
that the matter thereof was so indecent, irreligious, and improper that his proof-
reader--a young lady--had with difficulty been induced to continue its perusal."[10]
Roman tended to side against his young editor, but Harte "at once informed the
publisher that the question of the propriety of the story was no longer at issue:

the only question was of his capacity to exercise the proper editorial judgment; and that unless he was permitted to test that capacity by the publication of the story, and abide squarely by the result, he must resign his editorial position." The publisher yielded and "The Luck of Roaring Camp" was published, not without criticism from the religious community. Bret Harte's persistence and self-confidence paid off, for not long after that he received a letter from the ATLANTIC MONTHLY addressed to the "Author of 'The Luck of Roaring Camp'" requesting a similar story for that prestigious eastern periodical. Harte remained editor of the OVERLAND until December 1870, and his reputation, now national, grew apace. Of Harte's departure for the East in February 1871, biographer Henry Childs Merwin noted, "Seventeen years before he had landed there, a mere boy, without money or prospects, without trade or profession. Now he was the most distinguished person in California, and his departure marked the close of an epoch for that State."[11]

Editorial work seemed to have been congenial and beneficial to William Dean Howells too. In 1866, at 29 years of age, he went to Boston to take an appointment as assistant editor of the ATLANTIC MONTHLY, and in 1871 the former midwesterner became editor of this magazine, which was the voice of literary New England. Howells remained editor for ten years, and the literary figures with whom he became acquainted during that time impressed and influenced him, as he revealed later in LITERARY FRIENDS AND ACQUAINTANCE: A PERSONAL RETROSPECT OF AMERICAN AUTHORSHIP. He expressed relief when his editorship ended, but the drudgery necessarily involved in editing a prestigious literary periodical seems not really to have bothered him, even though he read all submitted manuscripts, wrote personal replies, and even proofread all material and double-checked all references. In a reminiscence of his editorship written in 1907, he said: "Not only the proofs were a pleasing and profitable drudgery, but the poor manuscripts, except in the most forbidding and hopeless instances, yielded their little crumbs of comfort; they supported while they fatigued. Very often they startled the drooping intelligence with something good and new amidst their impossiblity...."[12] And of the better manuscripts he said, "To feel the touch never felt before, to be the first to find the planet unimagined in the illimitable heaven of art, to be in at the dawn of a new talent, with the light that seems to mantle the written page: who would not be an editor, for such a privilege?"

Howells' success as ATLANTIC's editor resulted, though, from more than enjoyment of manuscript reading and an ability to make friends. He influenced the magazine's policies and character in a profound way and was himself influenced in turn. The editor himself later modestly claimed that "The magazine was already established in its traditions when I came to it, and when I left it fifteen years later it seemed to me that if I had done any good it was little more than to fix it more firmly in them."[13] But he understated his influence, for during his stay the ATLANTIC became increasingly national in scope. He accepted contributions from writers throughout the country, including the South and West, in greater numbers than had any previous editor.[14] On the other hand the periodical also affected the views and ideals of its editor, as Robert L. Hough has pointed out in THE QUIET REBEL: WILLIAM DEAN HOWELLS AS SOCIAL COMMENTATOR: "As the years passed it became increasingly evident that by the very fact of editing a journal of 'science, art, and politics,' Howells was forced to reflect upon contemporary problems. Of course there is no evidence to show that he was not being immersed in current events through other means, but the ATLANTIC was undoubtedly a great stimulus to his thinking."[15] Hough's study shows Howells with a greater social consciousness after his editorship. The editor's own reminiscence revealed a less tangible but nevertheless strong impression made on him during those ten years: "When the burden dropped from me, it was instantly as if I had never felt it. I did not think of it enough to miss it, to rejoice that it was gone. After another fifteen years I began to dream of resuming it. I would dream that I was on the train from New York to Boston, going back to be editor of the ATLANTIC again."[16]

Their associations with literary journals thus proved successful and beneficial to Howells and Harte, in contrast to the less satisfactory enterprises of Poe throughout his career, Emerson on THE DIAL, and Lowell on THE PIONEER. The roles played by such publications in the lives of major writers were, then, certainly not all disappointing. And yet such disappointments as those of Poe, Emerson, and Lowell may nevertheless be due to a general weakness or limitation in the American literary journal itself. Lowell, as we have seen, expected his publication to offer "a healthy and manly" literature as an alternative to the "trash" otherwise available. Poe expected to judge literature objectively according to "the purest rules of Art," never wavering from this ideal, and he was disgusted with the periodicals he worked on which did not aim loftily. Perhaps these men demanded more than their literary journals could achieve, especially if one considers both the hard work involved in editing a periodical and the need for popular support in order for these publications to survive. THE DIAL also seems to have been a victim of the excessively great expectations of those who founded it. On the one hand they wanted it to reflect their Transcendental philosophy, and on the other they were disappointed with its poor sales. According to George Willis Cooke it was precisely THE DIAL's originality that caused its doom:

> It took a new course, and one that was not only original, but initiative of better things in the future. It was a novelty, its freshness of tone, its romantic temper, its boundless hope and courage, that caused it to be criticized and jeered at generally by the more conservative literary journals. It was not conformatory enough to the old methods to secure it a general recognition on the part of the public; and it was condemned because it was not understood or appreciated.[17]

Success in the periodical field seems in fact to have been incompatible with lofty idealism. Harte's interest in local color fiction and Howells' enjoyment in discovering new writing talent are pursuits more in keeping with the limited reaches of the literary journals for which they labored.

Quality, Idealism, and Popularity

Lowell's comments in his PIONEER "Prospectus" and Poe's complaints about GRAHAM's and other periodicals are examples of another striking characteristic seen in nineteenth-century literary journals--the conflict between those who aimed at literary quality or pursued an ideal, and those whose major goal was financial

success. The most well-known example of this conflict is demonstrated in the
1890's, when the "cheap" periodicals (magazines), most prominently MCCLURE's
and MUNSEY's, arose to challenge the older, established, and complacent "qualities," including HARPER'S MONTHLY, the ATLANTIC MONTHLY, and the
CENTURY. To a great extent the "cheap" magazines were cheap in price only,
and offered a serious challenge precisely because their quality did rival that of
the older periodicals. But the very terms used by critics to describe this rivalry indicate the prevailing view that class periodicals were being threatened by
unprincipled journalistic opportunism. What is interesting here is not which side
was right, but that this conflict is only one of a number between various groups
of journals that occurred throughout the period covered in this bibliography. The
specific issues of contention of course changed over the years, but the resent-
ment of publications that considered themselves of "quality" toward those they
considered unprincipled is general throughout the century.

The first such conflict, beginning as early as the 1790's, involved periodicals
that supported the movement for American literary nationalism, a movement which
led to, and is sometimes mistakenly considered to begin with, Emerson's "American
Scholar" address of 1837. As William Free pointed out, THE COLUM-
BIAN MAGAZINE, a monthly founded in Philadelphia in 1786 and lasting until
1792, was backed by men who wanted American literature to cease its slavish
imitation of English writers.[18] Dedicated to this goal, the magazine solicited
contributions from American writers, was the first to pay for its articles, and
achieved the largest circulation of any eighteenth-century periodical. But finally the ideals proved too demanding, as was often the case during the next
century as well. The costs of publishing the periodical and paying for material
were never met by sales, and acceptable material was extremely difficult to
find. William Free also noted that "The history of the venture traveled a path
of disappointed hopes and frustrated ambitions."[19] The magazine struggled on
for six years, and, Free observed, "Had profit alone spurred the owners, the
COLUMBIAN would probably have failed after a few months as did so many of
its contemporaries. But the owners accepted the eschewal of profit as concomi-
tant with their mission to further the intellectual and cultural life of the nation,
and they continued in spite of the loss."[20] And they continued in spite of the
activities of other literary journals as well; Free observed that "Most of the
other magazines of the period stole....from one another and from English periodicals. But the COLUMBIAN attempted to realize its promise to print the best
original American pieces available."[21] As Free demonstrated, none of these
publications was really very successful anyway, but even here one can see the
conflict between periodicals dedicated to an ideal in literature and those in the
majority for which ideals and quality, at least original quality, were minor con-
cerns. After the War of 1812 the movement for literary nationalism grew apace,
with even the conservative NORTH AMERICAN REVIEW, founded in 1815, philo-
sophically supporting native work. One journal which undertook a campaign
for this difficult goal was John Neal's PORTICO, a Baltimore monthly started
in January 1816. A study of THE PORTICO has revealed that, "Never pretend-
ing to be dispassionate or impartial, the Baltimore magazine had axes to grind,
and ground them gleefully from the outset."[22] Neal willingly worked without
pay because of his dedication to the promotion of native literature. But THE
PORTICO failed only two years later in 1818. The interest in literary nationalism continued to grow, but the cases of THE COLUMBIAN and THE PORTICO are

early illustrations of short-lived publications dedicated to an ideal as contrasted to those in the majority dedicated to success in the marketplace.

The periodicals that did prosper financially, however, did so with a shrewd sense of what their readers wanted--not expressions of idealistic policies, but literature of general appeal, preferably that steeped in sentimentality. By far the most successful sentimental periodical of the nineteenth century was GODEY'S LADY'S BOOK, edited from 1837 by Sarah Josepha Hale. She retired in 1877, but the LADY'S BOOK itself survived, mostly on the momentum of its earlier phenomenal success, until 1898. Among the contributors in the early years were such notables as Edgar Allan Poe, Nathaniel Parker Willis, William Gilmore Simms, and George Pope Morris. Mrs. Hale and Louis Godey in fact insisted on printing the work of American authors, and thus even though their material was predominantly sentimental, they did take part in the movement for an independent national literature. Mrs. Hale also worked diligently for the improvement of women's status in American society. However, the publication's success was not due to these ideals, but to a conscious appeal to popular taste. In a comparison of GODEY'S to the modern woman's magazine, Ruth E. Finley notes that in both are found "the same editorial policy of pleasing the quantity rather than the quality public, the same profuse use of art, the same circulation clubs, the same struggle to present the most popular authors--even the same tendency to keep the figures of advancing circulation before the reader's eye."[23] Poe might complain about the quality of such periodicals, but Godey and Mrs. Hale found that financial success was to be had with the right combination of principle and practicality.

The early HARPER'S MONTHLY MAGAZINE, a publication quite different from GODEY'S LADY'S BOOK, followed a similar success formula. Harper Brothers publishing house did not found the periodical because of noble aims and unrealistic ideals, but for economic reasons, with good financial results. In his study of THE MAGAZINE IN AMERICA, Algernon Tassin observed that "The success of HARPER'S had shown that such a magazine could be utilized as the most effective advertising machinery to make known a publisher's list."[24] In a chapter unflatteringly entitled "HARPER'S--the Converted Corsair," Tassin commented on its aims: "HARPER'S MAGAZINE, in short, intended to do on a wider basis only what Harper's Family Library had done--and bring as many kinds of English literary goods as possible to an American market."[25] In order to achieve this objective, described appropriately in such mercenary terms, HARPER'S reprinted English literary works, often without permission. "Addisonian in its morality and its sentimentality," Tassin declares, "it was--in the beginning--following in all other respects the well-beaten and safe path. Unlike PUTNAM'S and the ATLANTIC, it sought nothing new."[26] Later editors have defended this early policy. Henry Mills Alden declared in 1909 that HARPER'S was "doing the best thing any magazine could then do in spreading broadcast the treasures of Victorian literature," and Frederick Lewis Allen said in 1950 that the policy was necessary because of the great popularity of English literature in America, and the obscurity, or else snobbishness, of American authors.[27]

Whether justified or not, such practices were not received well in some quarters, including those of PUTNAM'S MONTHLY, a New York magazine founded in 1853. PUTNAM'S criticized HARPER'S for reprinting English literature, and established for itself a policy of encouraging American writers from all sections of the country. PUTNAM'S praised southern writers, among them John Pendleton Kennedy, and included in its remarkable list of contributors Longfellow, Thoreau, and James Russell Lowell.[28] Much later, a former PUTNAM'S reader looked back and said, "Was ever an American magazine launched under more brilliant literary auspices, or with a list of contributors so readily recognizable half a century later?"[29] But the periodical only lasted until 1857, when the firm failed and PUTNAM'S made, "in the eyes of the world at least, a rather inglorious end."[30] A second series began in 1868, espousing the same principles, and with such figures as Edmund Clarence Stedman, Richard Henry Stoddard, and Bayard Taylor as regular contributors. Circulation never went above 15,000, and the periodical merged with SCRIBNER'S MONTHLY in 1870. Tassin offered the cliquishness of PUTNAM'S writers as one reason for the failure. Another could be the intense competition for what good American literature was available, as well as the lack of an international copyright. But most interesting for this discussion, perhaps, is Tassin's description of PUTNAM'S "quixotic attempt to make a native literature."[31] This phrase could as easily apply to the early COLUMBIAN MAGAZINE and THE PORTICO, whose idealistic struggles parallel PUTNAM'S. This is not to say that the rival HARPER'S was not a high quality journal even before it changed its policies toward English literature. It is to say that "quixotic" endeavors appeared repeatedly throughout nineteenth-century literary journalism, from the COLUMBIAN to Lowell's PIONEER, Poe's STYLUS, THE DIAL, and PUTNAM'S, and their idealism is in sharp contrast to the shrewd practicality of such successes as GODEY'S LADY'S BOOK and HARPER'S MONTHLY, which gave the public what it wanted instead of trying to upgrade or change its taste.

Periodical Geography and Ideology

Another major characteristic of these literary journals, and one which is perhaps more surprising to the modern student, is their sectional or group partisanship and rivalry. The consistency with which such partisanship appears is in fact the main reason why I have organized this bibliography according to major areas of the country. A glance at the titles of many of these entries reveals also that scholars of the American literary journals have remarked upon and investigated their sectional characteristics and loyalty, for these characteristics make such publications rich mines for the study of history and culture.

The literary periodicals of New England clearly show this sectional consciousness, or even self-consciousness. There was at times an exclusivity expressed in them (including the ATLANTIC MONTHLY before the changes brought about by the outsider Howells) that was perhaps created by a sense of tradition going back to the early MONTHLY ANTHOLOGY AND BOSTON REVIEW, a tradition distinct from the activities of literary journalism in the rest of the country. Thomas Wentworth Higginson, a man himself closely associated with New England literature, expresses this sectional or even local orientation in his book OLD CAMBRIDGE. He considered Cambridge to have experienced three literary epochs, and as the starting dates for each he used the appearances of THE NORTH

AMERICAN REVIEW in 1815, THE DIAL in 1840, and the ATLANTIC MONTHLY in 1857. The surprisingly local flavor of these major literary periodicals is evident in Higginson's statement that "nearly all the editors and most of the larger contributors were either natives of Cambridge or at some time residents there, apart from their mere college training."[32] Higginson was himself a Cambridge man, though, and snobbishness might appear to bias his views here. But his views do not really differ from those of modern scholars, who have repeatedly found sectional differences in the opinions and policies of literary journals. Albert Rabinovitz's study, "Criticism of French Novels in Boston Magazines: 1830-1860," serves as a typical case. After examining the views of a number of periodicals Rabinovitz concluded,

> The reactions of Boston magazine critics toward the most popular French novels of their day present more than a sentimental and historical interest. It is no secret that French novels did not meet with general approval in the United States from 1830 to 1860. But it is equally clear that the opinions of Boston reviewers on that particular subject did not fall into the conventional mold....The criticism of French novels in Boston magazines has worn well because it was liberal--much more so indeed than that of other sections of the country--to begin with.[33]

These sectional differences, then, are not mere matters of local pride; they include differences in literary and cultural values. Rabinovitz's article also demonstrates how literary periodicals can be used as sources for these values. Not only does he find useful criticism of French literature, but he discovers that the "conventional" modern generalization about the American reaction to French writers during this period is not totally correct, and at the same time he locates a little-known New England cultural attitude.

Many journals also speak for specific groups or literary movements within areas of the country, and again New England publications show this tendency clearly. THE MONTHLY ANTHOLOGY AND BOSTON REVIEW, as already noted, helped Boston to become a literary center. It was founded in 1805 by the Anthology Society, a group of intellectuals with a distinct set of literary and even political values, much as was to be the case with the scholarly and conservative NORTH AMERICAN REVIEW in 1815, considered to be THE MONTHLY ANTHOLOGY's successor. The journal's adherence to a single view of things in fact enables Lewis P. Simpson to draw a portrait of THE FEDERALIST LITERARY MIND by collecting various of THE MONTHLY ANTHOLOGY's articles from throughout its career. Forty years later another and more famous literary and philosophical movement, Transcendentalism, provided the inspiration for an entire group of literary periodicals, most of them, again, in New England. Not only THE DIAL, but THE BOSTON QUARTERLY REVIEW, THE HARBINGER, the AESTHETIC PAPERS, and THE MASSACHUSETTS QUARTERLY REVIEW were started by and expressed the views of Transcendentalists, and the contents of these and other magazines are examined individually in Clarence Gohdes' important study, THE PERIODICALS OF AMERICAN TRANSCENDENTALISM. Perhaps the most famous New England magazine founded by a distinct literary group was the ATLANTIC MONTHLY, established in 1857. Members of this group included such Brahmins as James Russell Lowell and Charles Eliot Norton, as well as Oliver Wendell Holmes, who named the publication and contributed his "Autocrat of the Break-

fast-Table" to it.[34] Higginson in his reminiscent CHEERFUL YESTERDAYS recounts the ATLANTIC's first publication in a chapter significantly entitled "The
Birth of a Literature," and his evaluation of the importance of the magazine's
circle of writers is indicated in his statement that "the essential fact is that in
this movement American literature was born. or. if not born,--for certainly Irving and Cooper had preceded,--was at least set on its feet."[35] This assessment
is probably wrong, but it does show the identification of periodicals with literary
groups or movements, an identification that makes the periodicals rich sources
for the investigation of literary history.

Partisanship reaches an extreme in the New York literary wars of the mid-nineteenth century which enmeshed Poe and Melville. The journals became weapons
in the hands of the combatants. The old guard Knickerbocker group controlled
the WHIG REVIEW, THE NEW YORK REVIEW, Nathaniel P. Willis' NEW YORK
MIRROR, and Lewis Gaylord Clark's KNICKERBOCKER MAGAZINE. An op-
posing group called "Young America," led by Evert Duyckinck and advocating
literary nationalism, spoke through the ARCTURUS and the DEMOCRATIC RE-
VIEW. In THE RAVEN AND THE WHALE, Perry Miller portrayed a rivalry so
vindictive that when the publishers Wiley, Putnam, and Appleton founded THE
LITERARY WORLD in 1847, men weary of the fight on both sides looked forward
to a new publication free from the old entanglements: "This was a brutal age
(for all that we suppose it decorously Victorian), and New York was a world
capitol of invective; yet men in all camps--some of whom had instincts of gen-
tility--were as weary of faction as they seemed powerless to extricate themselves from it. Suppose the LITERARY WORLD should become a vehicle of
truly nonfactional, scholarly, sophisticated criticism?"[36] For awhile these hopes
seemed to have been justified, but in the end Duyckinck, who had been hired
as editor, managed to change the periodical into a mouthpiece for Young America, and the publishers finally sold it to Evert and his brother George in 1848.
These controversies were not confined to two factions, though. A few years before the appearance of THE LITERARY WORLD, Robert Walsh, a Philadelphian
who edited THE NATIONAL GAZETTE AND LITERARY REGISTER, and then THE
AMERICAN QUARTERLY REVIEW from 1827 to 1836, was already attacking the
Knickerbocker group. Unlike the later Young Americans, he criticized the
Knickerbocker's modernism from the point of view of neoclassicism, the same
critical tenet held by the earlier COLUMBIAN MAGAZINE and PORTICO.[37]

These journalistic rivalries are not merely historical or cultural curiosities though,
because they affected major writers in ways which scholars should not ignore.
THE RAVEN AND THE WHALE itself shows such a relationship when Miller examines the effect of these rivalries on Herman Melville's literary fortunes. He
finds a weakness in studies that ignore the writer's New York literary milieu:
"Biographers of Melville work on a herocentric system that takes no heed of
circumstance; they imagine these visits, in the midst of this maelstrom, devoted
only to quiet conversation."[38] By ignoring this background to Melville's activities these biographers omit an essential dimension from their studies:

> In the history of Melville's reputation, the facts that he was publish-
> ed under the aegis of Evert Duyckinck and was damned by Lewis
> Gaylord Clark are footnotes, hardly worth mention. But for Melville,
> these facts were of immense initial importance, and became of in-

creasing importance in his development....He came as a lamb to the slaughter, with no suspicion that the city of New York was a literary butcher shop.[39]

Sidney P. Moss makes a similar point in POE'S LITERARY BATTLES: THE CRITIC IN THE CONTEXT OF HIS LITERARY MILIEU. Poe's literary criticism has for many the reputation of being inconsistent and vindictive, but these views, according to Moss, result from modern critics' "refusal to recognize that Poe's criticism had a context, the context of journalism, and that he had causes at stake, victories for which could not be wrested in a study."[40] Many of Poe's views and activities, including his dream of a strong and independent STYLUS, reflect his involvement in journalistic factionalism. Miller and Moss both use literary journals, not only to find information about literary groups or the culture of different areas of the country, but also to examine the cultural milieu of important writers whose works or lives might otherwise be misunderstood.

Sectional consciousness, if not group factionalism, is expressed in southern and western literary journals as well. Southern editors were self-consciously aware of the need to promote their area's literature, and periodicals such as RUSSELL'S MAGAZINE from 1857 to 1860 under Paul Hamilton Hayne and THE SOUTHERN LITERARY MESSENGER throughout its unusually long career from 1834 to 1864 published local literature and defended southern values. A passage from the editorial in the MESSENGER's first issue of August 1834 demonstrates the motivation of Thomas W. White, its founder: "Are we doomed forever to a kind of vassalage to our northern neighbors--a dependence for our literary food upon our brethren, whose superiority in all the great points of character,--in valor, eloquence, and patriotism,--we are in no wise disposed to admit?"[41] The periodical held more or less to this view throughout the editorships of Poe, White himself, Benjamin Blake Minor, John R. Thompson, and finally secessionist George W. Bagby. Post-war literary journals expressed similar sectional feelings. For example, THE SOUTHERN BIVOUAC, founded in Louisville in 1882, promoted southern literature, and so did SCOTT'S MONTHLY MAGAZINE, started in 1865 and offering encouragement to author Paul Hamilton Hayne.

Southern sectionalism in literary journals is not surprising, considering the general antagonism toward the North throughout the century. More remarkable, however, is the extent to which western periodicals promoted local culture and literature. One might expect that western editors, unlike their southern counterparts who felt the need for literary independence from the North, would emulate the work of New York, Philadelphia, and Boston editors. Some did of course, but most of the best ones took pride in their new local cultures and strove to assert their areas' uniqueness. For instance, THE OVERLAND MONTHLY of San Francisco was intended by publisher Anton Roman to mirror life in California. Although editor Bret Harte clashed with Roman when he did mirror local life in "The Luck of Roaring Camp," his fame was in fact achieved through the local color fiction he published in the MONTHLY in accord with the publication's general policy. Herbert Fleming remarks on this sense of pride in his long and detailed study of Chicago literary periodicals. Those of the 1840's and 1850's, he said, especially portray "the picture of the prairies and the expression of the western Zeitgeist."[42] Their names, like those of southern journals, show their orientation: the GEM OF THE PRAIRIE, the WESTERN MAGA-

ZINE, the CHICAGO MAGAZINE: THE WEST AS IT IS. The western journalists found almost no market for their products in the East, but found instead that "while the people of the states east of Illinois wish to know of the West, they want a literary presentation of western life made from their own point of view."[43] Undoubtedly this point of view did not include the literary and cultural integrity for which westerners were striving. Although post-Civil War periodicals tended to be more nationalistic, Chicago's LAKESIDE MONTHLY, "which stands today as the most notable in the city's literary history" according to Fleming, fostered local talent even though it was started as late as 1870. Originally entitled THE WESTERN MONTHLY, the journal was edited by Francis Fisher Browne, later editor of the Chicago DIAL. Fleming stated that "Mr. Browne tried always to get material that was indigenous, racy of the soil, expressive of the fertility and virility of the Mississippi Valley."[44] In 1873, just as the LAKESIDE began to make money, a financial panic hit, and Browne had a nervous breakdown. Ironically, and symptomatic of trends in literary periodicals, SCRIBNER'S MONTHLY, a big eastern publication consciously national in scope, offered to consolidate with, really to absorb, the LAKESIDE. Brown refused and the journal died.

The era of literary periodicals oriented toward particular geographical areas or literary groups seems to have ended at about this time, and the prosperity of SCRIBNER'S MONTHLY, later the CENTURY, is a major indication of this trend. Roswell Smith, who ran the business side of the operation, developed distribution techniques upon which national circulation and national reputation were based, while at the same time editor Josiah Gilbert Holland steered the periodical toward national views, the most remarkable example being his encouragement of southern veteran officers to contribute their versions to the Civil War series, a feature so popular that it almost doubled the CENTURY's circulation. Even the ATLANTIC MONTHLY, originally a bastion of brahminism, was changing to a more national outlook during the 1870's under Howells' direction. The only sizeable reaction against this trend occurred in the 1890's when little magazines such as THE CHAP-BOOK, THE LARK, THE PHILISTINE and M'LLE NEW YORK appeared in various places throughout the country. However, the real threats to the nationally-oriented "qualities"--the CENTURY, SCRIBNER'S MAGAZINE, the ATLANTIC MONTHLY, and HARPER'S MONTHLY--were not the little magazines but the MCCLURE'S, MUNSEY'S, and COSMOPOLITAN group, which improved circulation techniques, used national advertising, and were national in scope. The local flavor of the nineteenth-century literary journal, so long a dominating characteristic, had by this time all but disappeared. The nationally oriented magazines are, however, as well valuable sources for the student of literature or history. Robert Underwood Johnson, editor of the CENTURY from 1909 to 1913, reminiscing of his earlier associations with the periodical, asserted that "No history of the United States from a sociological point of view can be accurate or complete that does not take account of the part played in the development of the country after the war by this magazine and, later, by others which it stimulated."[45]

Scholars whose works are included in this bibliography have shown, however, that literary journals, including a number beyond those mentioned thus far, are mines of information in a variety of ways. They can reveal literary trends or gradual changes in attitude which are not easily discovered from other sources. Scott Holland Goodnight and Martin Henry Haertel use them for this purpose in their studies GERMAN LITERATURE IN AMERICAN MAGAZINES PRIOR TO 1846 and GERMAN LITERATURE IN AMERICAN MAGAZINES, 1846 TO 1880. A survey of magazines which were read by a wide public reveals more about the general trends of American awareness and acceptance of German literature than would a study of the works of individual writers. Similarly, Theodore P. Greene uses literary journals to trace changes in Zeitgeist in AMERICAN HEROES: THE CHANGING MODELS OF SUCCESS IN AMERICAN MAGAZINES. By comparing images of the American hero found in THE COLUMBIAN and MONTHLY ANTHOLOGY to those found in later magazines, including the CENTURY, MC-CLURE'S, and MUNSEY'S, he is able to draw conclusions about changing cultural ideas. Other possibilities offered by the literary journals as reflectors of cultural traits, ideas, and trends undoubtedly yet remain to be investigated.

The Bibliography: Scope and Limitations

I have already noted that the vast numbers of literary journals founded throughout the late eighteenth and nineteenth centuries make it necessary for me to limit this bibliography to only a part of the whole. Initially, of course, I have had to consider whether or not a particular publication was literary and could be defined as a journal or periodical. The first determination was not always easy, since many periodicals, including for instance the ATLANTIC, published articles on political and sociological issues, and have been called general publications by some critics. I have, however, included periodicals in which literature--fiction, poetry, and philosophical, critical, or familiar essays--was a primary element, as well as those which played parts in the development of American literary history. The WHIG REVIEW and the DEMO-CRATIC REVIEW are examples of the last. Arbitrarily, I have defined and included as journals or periodicals publications appearing no more frequently than once a week, no more infrequently than once a quarter. This yardstick eliminates both daily publications and yearly publications, including almanacs and gift books, such as Nathaniel Hawthorne's TOKEN, which in form and intent differs significantly from journals. But even within this definition there are many more publications than can be handled here, so I have included individual sections only on those which have been the subject of books, chapters in books, or articles. I have mentioned in annotations other literary journals which are discussed at length in the more general studies. There are also a few journals which, though not literary under my definition, published significant literary material, notably THE NATION. Instead of compiling a bibliography of secondary sources concerning these journals, many of which do not deal with literary matters, I have included an appendix of material dealing only with the literary aspects of these publications.

The year 1900 is not an arbitrary cutoff point for this study, but is appropriate because of changes in the field which occurred at about this time. The "quality" periodicals which had achieved success in the 1870's and 1880's were challenged by the new cheaper periodicals, such as MCCLURE'S and MUNSEY'S in the 1890's, and this challenge, combined with the rise of the little magazines, brought a new era in the life of the literary journal at the turn of the century. The periodicals which appeared just before 1900 but were continued into the twentieth century, including MCCLURE'S, MUNSEY'S, and REEDY'S MIRROR, will have individual sections devoted to them in a second volume, covering the period from 1900 to 1950. Of course some journals were published well before 1900 and continued well past that date, notably HARPER'S MONTHLY and the ATLANTIC MONTHLY, as well as the Chicago DIAL, the career of which is split almost evenly between the nineteenth and twentieth centuries. I have included sections on these magazines in this volume, and will include sections on them in the second, with different entries according to the time period covered.

Finally, I have collected the studies of Poe's journalistic activities in a second appendix. So much scholarly attention has been directed at this aspect of Poe's career, and he is such a prominent figure in nineteenth-century literary journalism, that I felt it appropriate to group this material in a separate, final section.

NOTES: INTRODUCTION

1.   W.H. Venable, BEGINNINGS OF LITERARY CULTURE IN THE OHIO VALLEY (1891; rpt. New York: Peter Smith, 1949), p. 58; John T. Flanagan, "Early Literary Periodicals in Minnesota," MINNESOTA HISTORY, 26 (1945), 294.

2.   Herbert Fleming, "The Literary Interests of Chicago," AMERICAN JOURNAL OF SOCIOLOGY, 11 (1905), 378.

3.   Frank Luther Mott, A HISTORY OF AMERICAN MAGAZINES, 1741-1850 (Cambridge: Belknap Press of Harvard University Press, 1957), I, 342.

4.   Lewis P. Simpson, ed., THE FEDERALIST LITERARY MIND: SELECTIONS FROM THE MONTHLY ANTHOLOGY AND BOSTON REVIEW, 1803-1811, INCLUDING DOCUMENTS RELATING TO THE BOSTON ATHENEUM (Baton Rouge: Louisiana State University Press, 1962), p. 40.   He expresses a similar view in "A Literary Adventure of the Early Republic: The Anthology Society and the MONTHLY ANTHOLOGY," NEW ENGLAND QUARTERLY, 27 (1954), 190.

5.   This address is included in M.A. DeWolfe Howe's "The Anthology Society and Its Minutes," JOURNAL OF THE PROCEEDINGS OF THE SOCIETY WHICH CONDUCTS THE MONTHLY ANTHOLOGY AND BOSTON REVIEW, OCTOBER 3, 1805, TO JULY 2, 1811 (Boston: The Boston Atheneum, 1910), pp. 24-25.

6.   George Willis Cooke, AN HISTORICAL AND BIOGRAPHICAL INTRODUCTION TO ACCOMPANY THE DIAL AS REPRINTED IN NUMBERS FOR THE ROWFANT CLUB (Cleveland: Rowfant Club, 1902), I, 68-108.

7.   J.F.A. Pyre, "The 'Dial' of 1840-45," THE DIAL, 26 (1899), 297.

8.   James Russell Lowell, ed., THE PIONEER: A LITERARY MAGAZINE (New York: Scholars' Facsimiles & Reprints, 1947), p. xxxvi.

9.   Quoted in Lewis P. Simpson, "Poe's Vision of His Ideal Magazine" in THE MAN OF LETTERS IN NEW ENGLAND AND THE SOUTH: ESSAYS ON THE HISTORY OF THE LITERARY VOCATION IN AMERICA (Baton Rouge: Louisiana State University Press, 1973), p. 135.

10. "General Introduction," THE WRITINGS OF BRET HARTE (Boston: Houghton, Mifflin, 1899), I, xiii-xiv. Harte relates the entire episode here.

11. Henry Childs Merwin, THE LIFE OF BRET HARTE: WITH SOME ACCOUNT OF THE CALIFORNIA PIONEERS (Boston: Houghton, Mifflin, 1911), p. 219.

12. William Dean Howells, "Recollections of an ATLANTIC Editorship," ATLANTIC, 100 (1907), 598.

13. Ibid., p. 595.

14. Van Wyck Brooks, HOWELLS: HIS LIFE AND WORLD (New York: E.P. Dutton, 1959), pp. 91-96.

15. Robert L. Hough, THE QUIET REBEL (Lincoln: University of Nebraska Press, 1959), p. 22.

16. Howells, p. 606.

17. George Willis Cooke, AN HISTORICAL AND BIOGRAPHICAL INTRODUCTION TO ACCOMPANY THE DIAL (Cleveland: Rowfant Club, 1902), I, 56.

18. The struggle of this group to achieve its goal is studied in depth by Free in THE COLUMBIAN MAGAZINE AND AMERICAN LITERARY NATIONALISM (The Hague: Mouton, 1968).

19. Ibid., p. 16.

20. Ibid., p. 17.

21. Ibid., p. 36.

22. Marshall W. Fishwick, "The PORTICO and Literary Nationalism After the War of 1812," WILLIAM AND MARY QUARTERLY, 8 (1951), 241.

23. Ruth E. Finley, THE LADY OF GODEY'S: SARAH JOSEPHA HALE (Philadelphia: J.B. Lippincott, 1931), pp. 60-61.

24. Algernon Tassin, THE MAGAZINE IN AMERICA (New York: Dodd, Mead, 1916), p. 206.

25. Ibid., p. 240.

26. Ibid., p. 248.

27. Henry Mills Alden, "Editor's Study," HARPER'S MONTHLY, 119 (1909), 961; Frederick Lewis Allen, "HARPER'S MAGAZINE" 1850-1950: A CENTENARY ADDRESS (New York: Newcomen Society in North America, 1950), pp. 8-9.

28. Notley S. Maddox, "Literary Nationalism in PUTNAM'S MAGAZINE,

1853-1857," AMERICAN LITERATURE, 14 (1942), 121.

29. M.S., "The Old PUTNAM'S," PUTNAM'S MONTHLY AND THE CRITIC, 1 (1906), 5. Mott ranks PUTNAM'S among the best periodicals to have appeared up to that time (II, 421).

30. Algernon Tassin, THE MAGAZINE IN AMERICA (New York: Dodd, Mead, 1916), p. 215.

31. Ibid., p. 228.

32. Thomas Wentworth Higginson, OLD CAMBRIDGE (New York: Macmillan, 1900), p. 71.

33. Albert Rabinovitz, "Criticism of French Novels in Boston Magazines: 1830-1860," NEW ENGLAND QUARTERLY, 14 (1941), 503-4.

34. Edward Emerson relates the ATLANTIC's founding by this literary circle in THE EARLY YEARS OF THE SATURDAY CLUB, 1855-1870 (Boston: Houghton, Mifflin, 1918), pp. 11-20.

35. Thomas Wentworth Higginson, CHEERFUL YESTERDAYS (Boston: Houghton, Mifflin, 1898), p. 187.

36. Perry Miller, THE RAVEN AND THE WHALE: THE WAR OF WORDS AND WITS IN THE ERA OF POE AND MELVILLE (New York: Harcourt, Brace, 1956), p. 186.

37. Guy R. Woodall, "Robert Walsh's War with the New York Literati: 1827-1836," TENNESSEE STUDIES IN LITERATURE, 15 (1970), 25-47.

38. Miller, p. 200.

39. Ibid., pp. 6-7.

40. Sidney P. Moss, POE'S LITERARY BATTLES: THE CRITIC IN THE CONTEXT OF HIS LITERARY MILIEU (Durham, N.C.: Duke University Press, 1963), p. x.

41. Quoted in Robert D. Jacobs, "Campaign for a Southern Literature: the SOUTHERN LITERARY MESSENGER," THE SOUTHERN LITERARY JOURNAL, 2 (Fall 1969), 68.

42. Herbert Fleming, "The Literary Interests of Chicago," AMERICAN JOURNAL OF SOCIOLOGY, 11 (1905), 380.

43. Ibid., p. 385.

44. Ibid., p. 401.

45. Robert Underwood Johnson, REMEMBERED YESTERDAYS (Boston: Little, Brown, 1923), p. 82.

Chapter 2

GENERAL STUDIES

AND CONTEMPORARY VIEWS

Chapter 2

GENERAL STUDIES
AND CONTEMPORARY VIEWS

Alden, Henry Mills. "Editor's Study." HARPER'S MONTHLY, 104 (1901), 167-70.

> Alden predicts that the decline of serial publication in literary journals will continue.

_____. "Editor's Study." HARPER'S MONTHLY, 105 (1902), 313-16.

> Alden defends serial publication of novels because of the high literary quality of many works which could otherwise not appear in periodicals.

_____. "Editor's Study." HARPER'S MONTHLY, 106 (1903), 491-94.

> This rambling essay compares contemporary periodical literature with the popular sentimental fiction published earlier.

_____. "Editor's Study." HARPER'S MONTHLY, 114 (1906), 807-10.

> Alden briefly views literary periodicals and the major figures involved with them.

_____. "Editor's Study." HARPER'S MONTHLY, 114 (1907), 969-72.

> An editor considers the pros and cons of anonymity in periodicals.

_____. MAGAZINE WRITING AND THE NEW LITERATURE. New York: Harper and Brothers, 1908.

> Although this study covers both British and American periodical literature, chapters V through VIII discuss the American magazine and its audience. Most of the chapters in this book originated in Alden's "Editor's Study" column in HARPER'S MONTHLY.

Allen, Frederick Lewis. "The American Magazine Grows Up." ATLANTIC, 180 (November 1947), 77-82.

> Allen, editor of the ATLANTIC, surveys the literary periodical

field from the founding of his own publication ninety years earlier
to the present.

Allen, Frederick Lewis, William L. Chenery and Fulton Oursler. "American
Magazines, 1741-1941." BULLETIN OF THE NEW YORK PUBLIC LIBRARY,
45 (1941), 439-60.

> These three addresses were delivered on April 29, 1941, for an
> exhibition of various magazines by the library. Allen's address is
> the most pertinent. He discusses briefly the struggle of the HAR-
> PER'S-CENTURY-SCRIBNER'S-ATLANTIC group against the "cheap"
> magazines at the end of the nineteenth century.

"American Magazines." SPECTATOR, 31 August 1899, pp. 268-69.

> The writer asks why American illustrated magazines are more pros-
> perous than English magazines, even in England. Answers offered
> are favorable rates for American publications charged by the English
> post office, the American public's great support of magazines, and
> the energy and resourcefulness of American editors and publishers.

"American Periodicals." THE DIAL, 13 (1892), 203-4.

> In this "general survey of the American monthlies, the most notable
> fact is the absence of any review for a moment comparable with
> either of the three great English monthlies."

"American Periodicals." LITERARY WORLD, 14 (1883), 414-15.

> Contemporary magazines, most of them literary, are surveyed and
> compared.

Auser, Cortland P. NATHANIEL P. WILLIS. New York: Twayne, 1969.

> Willis' experiences as editor of THE AMERICAN MONTHLY MAGA-
> ZINE, THE CORSAIR, THE NEW YORK MIRROR, THE NEW MIR-
> ROR and THE HOME JOURNAL are discussed throughout this study
> of his career.

Beers, Henry A. NATHANIEL PARKER WILLIS. Boston: Houghton, Mifflin,
1885.

> Beers covers Willis' contribution to or editorship of the following
> literary periodicals: the ATLANTIC MONTHLY, THE CORSAIR,
> THE NEW YORK MIRROR and THE HOME JOURNAL.

Beer, Thomas. THE MAUVE DECADE: AMERICAN LIFE AT THE END OF THE
NINETEENTH CENTURY. New York: Alfred A. Knopf, 1926.

> Chapter VI on "The American Magazines" attacks the prudery and
> bad judgment of the so-called sophisticated literary journals of the
> 1890's. Beer maintains that S.S. McClure treated good writers

better than did Henry Mills Alden of HARPER'S MONTHLY.

Bohning, Elizabeth E. "The Nibelungenlied in 19th Century American Periodicals." GERMAN QUARTERLY, 28 (1955), 14-18.

> Although the number of periodicals she examines is small, Bohning concludes that "while almost complete ignorance of the NIBELUNGENLIED characterizes the first half of the century, a lively interest was displayed in the main trends of German criticism in the latter half of the century."

Boynton, Percy H. A HISTORY OF AMERICAN LITERATURE. 1919; rpt. New York: AMS Press, 1970.

> This study contains an "Index to Leading Nineteenth Century Periodicals" (pp. 487-501), which presents dates, editors and publishers, and short discussions of the periodicals' contents.

Bradsher, Earl L. MATHEW CAREY, EDITOR, AUTHOR AND PUBLISHER: A STUDY IN AMERICAN LITERARY DEVELOPMENT. New York: Columbia University Press, 1912.

> Pp. 4-9 cover Carey's founding of first THE COLUMBIAN MAGAZINE in October 1786, and then THE AMERICAN MUSEUM in January 1787, both of which ended in December 1792. The contents and contributors to both journals are discussed.

Bragdon, Claude. "The Purple Cow Period: the 'Dinkey Magazines' that Caught the Spirit of the Nineties." THE BOOKMAN, 69 (1929), 475-78.

> Bragdon, referred to during the period as "the Beardsley of America," remembers THE LARK, THE CHAP-BOOK, and THE PHILISTINE as the most important of the little magazines.

Bristed, Charles A. "The Periodical Literature of America." PIECES OF A BROKEN-DOWN CRITIC, PICKED UP BY HIMSELF. Baden-Baden: Scotzniovsky, 1859. III, 14-24.

> This Englishman concludes that "Considering the great demand for periodical literature in the New-World, one is surprised to find it so bad in point of quality." He blames this on the lack of adequate pay for contributors and the lack of an international copyright.

Cairns, William B. "Later Magazines." THE CAMBRIDGE HISTORY OF AMERICAN LITERATURE. Ed. William Peterfield Trent, et al. New York: Macmillan, 1921. III, 299-318.

> Cairns surveys developments since 1850 among literary periodicals.

————. "Magazines, Annuals, and Gift Books, 1783-1850." THE CAMBRIDGE

HISTORY OF AMERICAN LITERATURE. Ed. William Peterfield Trent, et al. New York: Macmillan, 1918. II, 160–75.

> Combined with the foregoing entry, this study provides a good short introduction to the literary periodical in America.

_____. ON THE DEVELOPMENT OF AMERICAN LITERATURE FROM 1815 TO 1833, WITH ESPECIAL REFERENCE TO PERIODICALS. Madison: University of Wisconsin Press, 1898.

> Many literary journals supported the concept of an American literature and attacked their contemporaries for neglecting it in favor of British literature. Cairns discusses periodicals from various areas of the country, and in thorough appendices lists those founded during this period, including dates, frequency of issue, editors, and publishers.

_____. "Periodicals and Annuals." BRITISH CRITICISMS OF AMERICAN WRITINGS, 1815–1833. Madison: University of Wisconsin Press, 1922. Pp. 280–87.

> This chapter consists predominantly of references and quotations from British periodicals commenting upon American journals and annuals. About half of the discussion deals with the reception of THE NORTH AMERICAN REVIEW, which was generally favorable.

Calkins, Earnest Elmo. "Magazine into Marketplace." SCRIBNER'S MAGAZINE, 1 (January 1937), 108–17.

> Calkins traces the rise of large-scale magazine advertising, from Fletcher Harper's feeling that it degraded the literature, through Roswell Smith's pioneering work for SCRIBNER'S MONTHLY, to the thirty pages of advertising published in the first issue of SCRIBNER'S MAGAZINE.

Cameron, Kenneth Walter. EMERSON'S WORKSHOP: AN ANALYSIS OF HIS READING IN PERIODICALS THROUGH 1836 WITH THE PRINCIPAL THEMATIC KEY TO HIS ESSAYS, POEMS, AND LECTURES. 2 vols. Hartford: Transcendental Books, 1964.

> Emerson's reading in both English and American periodicals is listed in the first volume. Also included is a list of the contents of THE ATHENEUM; OR, SPIRIT OF THE ENGLISH MAGAZINES, a reprint journal Emerson read regularly.

Chambers, Robert William. "The Influence of Magazine Journalists on the Rise of Realism in America, 1870–1890." Dissertation, University of Texas, 1964.

> During the height of their success before the rise of the cheap magazines, literary journals including HARPER'S, the ATLANTIC, and SCRIBNER'S MONTHLY-CENTURY fostered the realistic movement in fiction.

Chambers, Stephen, and G.P. Mohrmann. "Retoric in Some American Periodicals, 1815-1850." SPEECH MONOGRAPHS, 37 (1970), 435-59.

In order to study the attitudes toward rhetoric during this period, the authors examine selected periodicals, including THE NORTH AMERICAN REVIEW, THE KNICKERBOCKER, and THE SOUTHERN LITERARY MESSENGER.

Charvat, William. THE ORIGINS OF AMERICAN CRITICAL THOUGHT, 1810-1835. Philadelphia: University of Pennsylvania Press, 1936.

Although Charvat focuses on critical ideas, he examines literary periodicals in order to ascertain what ideas were current during the period. For instance, he notes that Philadelphia was one of the most conservative cities in terms of literary ideas and states that Joseph Dennie's THE PORT FOLIO, with its patrician outlook, was indicative of the dominant attitude there.

"Cheap Magazines." MCCLURE'S MAGAZINE, 5 (1895), 287-88; "The Ten-Cent Magazine Again." MCCLURE'S, 5 (1895), 383-84.

After having lowered its price to ten cents, MCCLURE'S favorably compares its own quality, and that of other new inexpensive magazines, to that of the established periodicals, the CENTURY, HARPER'S, the ATLANTIC, and SCRIBNER'S MAGAZINE.

"The Christmas Magazines and Literary Decay." POET-LORE, 5 (1893), 39-43.

The writer looks at various Christmas issues, including those of the ATLANTIC, THE FORUM, HARPER'S MONTHLY, the CENTURY, and SCRIBNER'S MAGAZINE, and concludes that, to varying degrees, the decorations mask a paucity of good literature.

Cohn, Jan. "The Negro Character in Northern Magazine Fiction of the 1860's." NEW ENGLAND QUARTERLY, 43 (1970), 572-92.

Although abolitionist in outlook, northern magazine literature of the 1860's revealed a complacent sense of white superiority.

Cook, Elizabeth, Christine. "Colonial Newspapers and Magazines, 1704-1775." THE CAMBRIDGE HISTORY OF AMERICAN LITERATURE. Ed. William Peterfield Trent, et al. New York: G.P. Putnam's Sons, 1917. I, 111-23.

Cook focuses on newspapers and the influence of English writers, specifically Pope and Addison, on early American writing. However, some information is provided about literary journals, especially William Smith's THE AMERICAN MAGAZINE.

_____. LITERARY INFLUENCES IN COLONIAL NEWSPAPERS, 1704-1750. New York: Columbia University Press, 1912.

During the period of the 1720's through the 1740's weekly news-

papers, primarily because of a scarcity of fresh news, became almost completely literary in content. As more news became available and monthly journals began to appear, the newspaper became
distinct from the literary periodical.

Davidson, H. Carter. "The Sonnet in Seven Early American Magazines and
Newspapers." AMERICAN LITERATURE, 4 (1932), 180-87.

After perusing such periodicals as THE COLUMBIAN MAGAZINE
and THE MASSACHUSETTS MAGAZINE, Davidson draws conclusions
about influences upon the form and content of early American son-
nets.

Davis, Edward Ziegler. TRANSLATIONS OF GERMAN POETRY IN AMERICAN
MAGAZINES, 1741-1810. Philadelphia: Americana Germanica Press, 1905.

Although his book consists primarily of the translations themselves,
Davis does establish in an introduction that the periodicals were
instrumental in bringing German literature to the American public's
attention. In addition he provides a list of prose translations and
the magazines in which they appeared.

Derby, J.C. FIFTY YEARS AMONG AUTHORS, BOOKS AND PUBLISHERS.
New York: G.W. Carleton & Co., 1884.

The founding and success of THE NEW YORK LEDGER are related
in Chapter IX, "Robert Bonner." The ATLANTIC's early years are
viewed in Chapter XIV, "H.O. Houghton--Houghton, Mifflin &
Co." Chapter XLIX on "Roswell Smith--The Century Co." covers
the planning, founding, and success of the CENTURY, and Chapter
XVI, "George Palmer Putnam," does the same for PUTNAM'S
MONTHLY.

Doyle, Mildred D. SENTIMENTALISM IN AMERICAN PERIODICALS, 1741-
1800. New York: New York University Press, 1944.

Duyckinck, Evert A. and George L. CYCLOPAEDIA OF AMERICAN LITERA-
TURE: EMBRACING PERSONAL AND CRITICAL NOTICES OF AUTHORS, AND
SELECTIONS FROM THEIR WRITINGS, FROM THE EARLIEST PERIOD TO THE
PRESENT DAY; WITH PORTRAITS, AUTOGRAPHS, AND OTHER ILLUSTRA-
TIONS. Ed. to date by M. Laird Simons. 2 vols. Philadelphia: T. Ellwood
Zell, 1875.

The careers of a number of magazine editors are sketched here.
The "Periodicals" entry in the "Index" lists publications covered.

Eaton, Charles Henry. "A Decade of Magazine Literature--1888-1897." THE
FORUM, 26 (1898), 211-16.

Eaton divides the articles in THE FORUM and NINETEENTH CEN-
TURY, an English journal, into different categories (politics, fiction,

etc.), and then generalizes not only about this type of journal but about the thought and culture of the American and English publics.

Ellis, Harold Milton. JOSEPH DENNIE AND HIS CIRCLE: A STUDY IN AMERICAN LITERATURE FROM 1792 TO 1812. Bulletin of the University of Texas No. 40. Austin: University of Texas, 1915.

Ellis examines Dennie's editing and writing activities for literary journals in the following chapters: Chapter V, "Boston, 1795-- THE TABLET," Chapter VI, "Walpole, 1795-1799--THE FARMER'S MUSEUM," and Chapters VIII through XI on THE PORT FOLIO. Appendices D and E list the dates of publication of Dennie's "Far- rago" and "Lay Preacher" essays, and the journal in which each appeared.

Ellsworth, Elmo, Jr. "Volume One, Number One." THE BOOKMAN, 72 (1930), 381-92.

This is a chatty and at times informative discussion of Ellsworth's collection of first numbers, some of them early or obscure journals.

Ellsworth, William Webster. A GOLDEN AGE OF AUTHORS: A PUBLISHER'S RECOLLECTION. Boston: Houghton, Mifflin, 1919.

Ellsworth was associated with the Century Company for almost forty years, and his recollections include material on Roswell Smith, J.G. Holland, and Richard Watson Gilder of THE CENTURY MAGA- ZINE, and individuals who worked on other periodicals of the time, including Mary Mapes Dodge of the ST. NICHOLAS.

Faxon, Frederick W. "American Literary Periodicals and Their Use in Libraries." LIBRARY JOURNAL, 59 (1934), 907-9.

An extremely short summary of literary periodical history is followed by a discussion of indexes, such as Poole's and Wilson's, and of current library holdings of and subscriptions to magazines.

Flewelling, H.L. "Critical Opinion in American Periodicals, 1780-1812." Dissertation, University of Michigan, 1932.

Floan, Howard R. THE SOUTH IN NORTHERN EYES, 1831 TO 1861. Austin: University of Texas Press, 1958.

In Chapter VI on "New England Magazines" Floan examines the attitudes of THE NORTH AMERICAN REVIEW, THE NEW ENGLAND MAGAZINE, and the WAVERLY MAGAZINE, a literary weekly. He discovers that "Whereas the major New England writers were for the most part either hostile or silent in respect to the South, there is evidence that these journals were both sympathetic and expressive in their treatment of it." Chapter VII, "New York Backgrounds," includes a discussion of PUTNAM'S MAGAZINE's

reasonable views of things southern and its objective attitude toward sectional conflicts.

Fogle, Richard H. "Organic Form in American Criticism: 1840-1870." THE
DEVELOPMENT OF AMERICAN LITERARY CRITICISM. Chapel Hill: University
of North Carolina Press, 1955. Pp. 75-111.

> In the course of his discussion Fogle examines the critical views of
> THE DIAL, the DEMOCRATIC REVIEW, the WHIG REVIEW, and
> THE NORTH AMERICAN REVIEW.

Garland, Hamlin. ROADSIDE MEETINGS. New York: Macmillan, 1930.

> In discussing "the purely literary side" of his life, Garland includes
> chapters on "The ARENA and Its Radicals,"The 'Chap-Book' and
> Its Writers," and "Old Editors and New Magazines." The last
> covers Garland's association with Gilder of the CENTURY, Alden
> of HARPER'S MONTHLY, S.S. McClure of MCCLURE'S, and others.

Garnsey, Caroline John. "Ladies' Magazines to 1850: The Beginnings of an
Industry." BULLETIN OF THE NEW YORK PUBLIC LIBRARY, 58 (1954), 74-
88.

> This study includes a checklist.

Garwood, Irving. AMERICAN PERIODICALS FROM 1850 TO 1860. Macomb:
Western Illinois State Teachers College, 1931.

> Garwood lists various types of magazines and discusses their histori-
> cal and literary importance. His final section, "Group VIII,"
> covers literary periodicals. This study originated as a dissertation
> written at the University of Chicago in 1922.

Gohdes, Clarence. AMERICAN LITERATURE IN NINETEENTH-CENTURY ENG-
LAND. New York: Columbia University Press, 1944.

> Chapter II, "The Periodicals," covers the invasion and influence of
> American literary periodicals in England throughout the century, as
> well as attempts on both sides of the Atlantic to establish an in-
> ternational journal. Gohdes reveals that HARPER'S MONTHLY and
> the CENTURY did so well in England that the work of some well-
> known English writers could be found only in their pages.

Goodnight, Scott Holland. GERMAN LITERATURE IN AMERICAN MAGAZINES
PRIOR TO 1846. Bulletin of the University of Wisconsin No. 188. Madison,
1907.

> The growing awareness of German literature is traced through Ameri-
> can literary periodicals. Goodnight includes an extensive bibliog-
> raphy of the titles used in his study.

Graham, Walter. "Notes on Literary Periodicals in America before 1800." WESTERN RESERVE UNIVERSITY BULLETIN, 20 (1927), 5-27.

Graham reviews the earliest American literary journals.

Greene, Theodore P. AMERICA'S HEROES: THE CHANGING MODELS OF SUCCESS IN AMERICAN MAGAZINES. New York: Oxford University Press, 1970.

This study investigates ideas in periodicals of the National Period, from 1787 to 1820, and compares them to ideas expressed in periodicals from 1894 to 1918 in order to determine changes that have occurred in America's views of individualism and success. Among the periodicals discussed in detail are THE COLUMBIAN MAGAZINE and THE MONTHLY ANTHOLOGY from the early period, and CENTURY, MCCLURE'S, MUNSEY'S, COSMOPOLITAN, COLLIER'S, and THE SATURDAY EVENING POST from the later.

Greenslet, Ferris. THE LIFE OF THOMAS BAILEY ALDRICH. Boston: Houghton, Mifflin, 1908.

Chapter VI covers Aldrich's editorship of the ATLANTIC, and pp. 28-31 deal with his early work on the periodicals of N.P. Willis, including his sub-editorship of THE HOME JOURNAL.

Grueningen, John Paul von. "Goethe in American Periodicals 1860-1900." PMLA, 50 (1935), 1155-64.

This study of the interest in Goethe, "despite all negative elements, reveals Goethe as the most imposing figure in German literature, as one of the greatest in world literature, and as a force comprising a distinct world of fertile thought in American civilization."

_____. "Goethe in American Periodicals from 1860 to 1900." Dissertation, University of Wisconsin, 1931.

Haertel, Martin Henry. GERMAN LITERATURE IN AMERICAN MAGAZINES, 1846 TO 1880. Bulletin of the University of Wisconsin No. 263. Madison, 1908.

This examination of literary journals reveals an interest in classical German writers from 1846 to 1853, a decline of interest from 1854 to 1868, and a renewed interest, this time in the German novelists, from 1869 to 1880.

Hamilton, Gail. "Magazine Literature." SKIRMISHES AND SKETCHES. Boston: Ticknor and Fields, 1866. Pp. 225-32.

Literature which appears in magazines is less permanent and lighter than that which is published in book form, but nevertheless has its own importance and does benefit the reading public.

Harding, Walter. "Some Forgotten Reviews of WALDEN." THOREAU SOCIETY BULLETIN, 46 (Winter 1954).

> Reviews of WALDEN from THE SOUTHERN LITERARY MESSENGER, THE NATIONAL MAGAZINE, and GRAHAM'S MAGAZINE are reprinted.

Hendrick, Burton J. THE TRAINING OF AN AMERICAN: THE EARLIER LIFE AND LETTERS OF WALTER H. PAGE, 1855-1913. Boston: Houghton, Mifflin, 1928.

> Chapter VII, "THE FORUM," covers Page's editorship, including his reasons for resigning, and a discussion of the journal's contents. Chapter VIII, "Boston and the 'Atlantic'," deals with his editorship of that magazine from 1895 to 1899.

Hoeber, Arthur A. "A Century of American Illustration." THE BOOKMAN, 8 (1898-1899), 213-19, 316-24, 429-39, 540-48.

> Hoeber touches upon illustrated periodicals such as HARPER'S MONTHLY and the CENTURY.

Holly, Flora Mai. "Notes on Some American Magazine Editors." THE BOOKMAN, 12 (1900), 357-68.

> Walter Hines Page, Bliss Perry, and Henry Mills Alden are among the fifteen editors discussed in short biographies.

Holman, Harriet R. "Magazine Editors and the Stories of Thomas Nelson Page's Late Flowering." ESSAYS MOSTLY ON PERIODICAL PUBLISHING IN AMERICA. Ed. James Woodress. Durham, N.C.: Duke University Press, 1973. Pp. 148-61.

> Conservative, overly-cautious magazine editors, except for those at SCRIBNER'S MAGAZINE, rejected Page's innovative stories because they felt more secure with the local-color fiction which had brought his initial success.

Howells, William Dean. "Editor's Easy Chair." HARPER'S MONTHLY, 114 (1907), 641-44.

> In a fictional dialogue between two poets, the poetic contents of unnamed earlier periodicals are compared to those of contemporary magazines. Although the comparison is generally unfavorable to the earlier literature, some of it is seen as valuable even though now forgotten.

_____. "Editor's Easy Chair." HARPER'S MONTHLY, 129 (1914), 476-78.

> Howells contends that HARPER'S and similar periodicals are no longer as purely literary as they had been when they were begun because the public now demands a greater diversity in content.

_____. LITERARY FRIENDS AND ACQUAINTANCE: A PERSONAL RETRO-
SPECT OF AMERICAN AUTHORSHIP. Ed. David F. Hiatt and Edwin H. Cady.
Bloomington: Indiana University Press, 1968.

Chapter II, "First Impressions of Literary New York," and Chapter
IV, "Literary Boston as I Knew It," reveal Howells' views of some
of the periodicals of those cities and the people involved with
them. Chapter IV covers the period of his ATLANTIC editorship.

_____. "The Editor's Relations With the Young Contributor." LITERATURE
AND LIFE. New York: Harper and Brothers, 1911. Pp. 63-77.

Howells advises the young contributor that he should not be discouraged by his difficulties, but consider them beneficial to his
literary career in the long run.

Hudson, Frederic. JOURNALISM IN THE UNITED STATES, FROM 1690 TO
1872. New York: Harper and Brothers, 1873.

Although newspapers are the main subject of this study, Hudson
includes short discussions of ladies' magazines (pp. 497-98) and
Bonner's THE NEW YORK LEDGER (pp. 646-55).

Ingraham, Charles A. "American Magazines, Past and Present." AMERICANA,
15 (1921), 325-34.

This article generally discusses past editors who "were ever ready
to immolate themselves on the altar of the republic of letters, to
heroically devote their lives and substance to the hopeless enterprise of maintaining a periodical devoted to 'polite literature.'"

Jaffe, Adrian H. "French Literature in American Periodicals, 1741-1800."
Dissertation, New York University, 1950.

_____. "French Literature in American Periodicals of the Eighteenth Century."
REVUE DE LITTERATURE COMPAREE, 38 (1964), 51-60.

Jaffe discusses the American interest in French scientific and political ideas, as well as French literature, shown in periodicals.

Johannsen, Albert. THE HOUSE OF BEADLE AND ADAMS AND ITS DIME
AND NICKEL NOVELS: THE STORY OF A VANISHED LITERATURE. 2 vols.
Norman: University of Oklahoma Press, 1950.

Publishing and editing histories of the following story magazines
from 1851 to 1897 are given on pp. 414-75 of Volume I: THE
YOUTH'S CASKET, THE HOME, BEADLE'S MONTHLY, the SATUR-
DAY JOURNAL, BEADLE'S WEEKLY (later called THE BANNER
WEEKLY), BELLES AND BEAUX, GIRL OF TODAY, THE NEW YORK
MIRROR, and THE YOUNG NEW YORKER. Further information on
them is included in "A History of the Firm," pp. 15-72 of Volume
I.

Joyeaux, Georges J. "French Fiction in American Magazines: 1800-1848." PROCEEDINGS OF THE IVth CONGRESS OF THE INTERNATIONAL COMPARATIVE LITERATURE ASSOCIATION. Fribourg, 1964. Ed. Francis Jost. The Hague: Mouton, 1967. II, 1175-83. This article was first published in the ARIZONA QUARTERLY, 21 (1965), 29-40.

> Joyeaux discusses the reception of French fiction by American literary journals.

_____. "French Thought in American Magazines, 1800-1848." Dissertation, Michigan State University, 1951.

Kilmer, Joyce. "Magazines Cheapen Fiction: George Barr McCutcheon." LITERATURE IN THE MAKING, BY SOME OF ITS MAKERS. 1945; rpt. Port Washington, N.Y.: Kennikat Press, 1968. Pp. 155-66.

> McCutcheon declares that "if we undertake to analyze the distinction between the first-class English writers of today and many of our Americans, we will find that their superiority resolves itself quite simply into the fact that they do not write their novels as serials."

King, Kimball. "Local Color and the Rise of the American Magazine." ESSAYS MOSTLY ON PERIODICAL PUBLISHING IN AMERICA. Ed. James Woodress. Durham, N.C.: Duke University Press, 1973. Pp. 121-33.

> This article explores the type of fiction popular in magazines during the period from after the Civil War to about 1900. The writer looks for the sociological causes of both the rise of local color fiction and the continued popularity of sentimental literature.

Kirkpatrick, John Ervin. TIMOTHY FLINT: PIONEER, MISSIONARY, AUTHOR, EDITOR, 1780-1840. Cleveland: Arthur H. Clark Co., 1911.

> From 1827 to 1830, while in Cincinnati, Flint edited THE WESTERN MONTHLY REVIEW (pp. 185-189); later he edited THE KNICKERBOCKER MAGAZINE for a short time (pp. 210-15).

Lamplugh, George R. "The Image of the Negro in Popular Magazine Fiction, 1875-1900." JOURNAL OF NEGRO HISTORY, 57 (1972), 177-89.

> Short stories during this period that appeared in the ATLANTIC, HARPER'S MONTHLY, SCRIBNER'S-CENTURY, and SCRIBNER'S MAGAZINE, many of them written by southern authors, portrayed the Negro and his social situation both before and after the Civil War in an unrealistic and complacent way.

"A Leaf From the American Magazine-Literature of the Last Century." ATLANTIC, 5 (1860), 429-38.

> This article discusses the contents of eighteenth-century magazines,

including a growing "class of publications which professed, while giving a proper share of attention to the important department of news, to occupy the field of literature rather than journalism, and to serve as a Museum, Depository, or Magazine of the polite arts and sciences." It examines in detail THE AMERICAN MAGAZINE AND HISTORICAL CHRONICLE, begun in 1743.

Lewis, Benjamin M. AN INTRODUCTION TO AMERICAN MAGAZINES, 1800-1810. University of Michigan Department of Library Sciences, No. 5. Ann Arbor, 1961.

This is the revised historical introduction to Lewis' bibliographical dissertation. Although various types of magazines are discussed, Chapter II on "The Magazine and American Culture, 1800-1810" focuses on a number of literary journals. Chapter I on "The Nature of American Magazines, 1800-1810" examines aspects of the publishing business and the economics of magazine work.

_____. "Engravings in American Magazines, 1741-1810." BOOKS IN AMERICA'S PAST: ESSAYS HONORING RUDOLPH H. GJELSNESS. Ed. David Kaser. Charlottesville: University of Virginia Press, 1966. Pp. 204-17.

Lewis discusses the quality and historical importance of the copper-plate engravings which were printed in periodicals of this period, including THE MASSACHUSETTS MAGAZINE.

Linneman, William Richard. "American Life as Reflected in Illustrated Humor Magazines: 1877-1900." Dissertation, University of Illinois, 1960.

Linneman investigates the policies and contents of such magazines as PUCK, JUDGE, TRUTH, THE WASP, TEXAS SIFTINGS, and THE ARKANSAW TRAVELER.

Linton, W.J. THE HISTORY OF WOOD-ENGRAVING IN AMERICA. Boston: Estes and Lauriat, 1882.

Chapters IV and VI briefly discuss the quality of engravings in illustrated periodicals including HARPER'S MONTHLY, the RIVERSIDE MAGAZINE, SCRIBNER'S MONTHLY, and ST. NICHOLAS.

Lovejoy, George Newell. "Half-Forgotten Magazines." CHAUTAUQUAN, 33 (1901), 28-30.

Histories of the following magazines are briefly surveyed: THE KNICKERBOCKER, THE AMERICAN MONTHLY, THE SOUTHERN LITERARY MESSENGER, GRAHAM'S, and PUTNAM'S.

Lowens, Irving. "Writings About Music in the Periodicals of American Transcendentalism (1835-50)." JOURNAL OF THE AMERICAN MUSICOLOGICAL SOCIETY, 10 (Summer 1957), 71-85.

This study includes a bibliography of magazine articles about music.

Lucey, William L. "Catholic Magazines: 1865-1900." RECORDS OF THE AMERICAN CATHOLIC HISTORICAL SOCIETY OF PHILADELPHIA, 63 (1952), 21-36, 85-109, 133-56, 197-223.

> Some of the magazines described in this survey were literary or semi-literary.

Lutwack, Leonard I. "The Dynamics of Conservative Criticism: Literary Criticism in American Magazines, 1880-1900." Dissertation, Ohio State University, 1950.

Marraro, Howard R. "Italian Culture in Eighteenth-Century American Magazines." ITALICA, 22 (1945), 21-31.

> Marraro investigates a number of periodicals in order to determine the extent to which Italian ideas and literature influenced American thought. He includes a list from these magazines of articles on Italian literature, translations of poetry and prose, literary imitations, and other works relating to Italian culture.

_____. "Rome and the Catholic Church in Eighteenth-Century American Magazines." CATHOLIC HISTORICAL REVIEW, 32 (1946), 157-89.

> Literary and political journals of the period generally reflected hostile views toward the Catholic Church.

Matthews, Brander. "American Magazines." THE BOOKMAN, 61 (1919), 533-41.

> In a rambling essay Matthews first calls for a good history of American monthly magazines and then reviews a number of monthlies and quarterlies of the past and present.

_____. "Confessions of a Septuagenarian Contributor." UNPARTIZAN REVIEW, 14 (1920), 97-108.

> THE GALAXY, HARPER'S MONTHLY, and the CENTURY are among the periodicals with which Matthews was associated, and he discusses them briefly here.

_____. "Some American Periodicals: Rambling Impressions of a Literary New Yorker." THE OUTLOOK, 117 (1917), 50-52, 56.

> In this familiar essay Matthews talks about the magazines and newspapers of the 1880's, and his own contributions to them.

Maurice, Arthur Bartlett. "Literary Magazines." AMERICAN WRITERS ON AMERICAN LITERATURE, BY THIRTY-SEVEN CONTEMPORARY WRITERS. New

York: Horace Liveright, 1931. Pp. 464-75.

This essay sketches the history of literary magazines.

McCloskey, John C. "The Campaign of Periodicals After the War of 1812 for National American Literature." PMLA, 50 (1935), 262-73.

A nationalistic attitude is expressed in THE ANALECTIC MAGA-ZINE, NILE'S REGISTER, and to some extent THE NORTH AMERI-CAN REVIEW and THE PORT FOLIO, among others. McCloskey focuses on THE PORTICO, a Baltimore periodical which promoted American literature.

Mencken, Henry L. "The American Magazine." PREJUDICES: FIRST SERIES. New York: Alfred A. Knopf, 1919. Pp. 171-80.

Mencken begins by criticizing Tassin's THE MAGAZINE IN AMERI-CA for being a badly-written though thorough study. He then sur-veys the field himself, concluding that the CENTURY was the best literary periodical to appear in the nineteenth century.

Monteiro, George. "Rudyard Kipling: Early Printings in American Periodicals." PAPERS OF THE BIBLIOGRAPHICAL SOCIETY OF AMERICA, 61 (1967), 127-28.

Among five works published in 1890 are four short stories reprinted by LITTELL'S LIVING AGE from the British MACMILLAN'S MAGA-ZINE.

Moore, Rayburn S. "The Magazine and the Short Story in the Ante-Bellum Period." SOUTH ATLANTIC BULLETIN, 38 (May 1973), 44-51.

Although most periodicals pandered to the mediocrity of public taste, "there were important exceptions, and the way was gradual-ly paved for the great age of the literary magazines after the war."

_____. "Paul Hamilton Hayne and Northern Magazines, 1866-1886." ESSAYS MOSTLY ON PERIODICAL PUBLISHING IN AMERICA. Ed. James Woodress. Durham, N.C.: Duke University Press, 1973. Pp. 134-47.

After the Civil War Hayne began publishing his poetry in northern magazines, and Moore studies Hayne's relationship with the four most prominent of these, LIPPINCOTT'S, SCRIBNER'S-CENTURY, HARPER'S MONTHLY, and the ATLANTIC. "Hayne's relations followed the pattern of initial acceptance and cordiality and sub-sequent rejection and antipathy."

Mott, Frank Luther. "American Magazines, 1865-1880." Dissertation, Colum-bia University, 1928.

_____. AMERICAN MAGAZINES, 1865-80. Iowa City: Midland Press,

1928.

This survey of the magazines of this period is comprehensive, but does not approach the depth and scholarship of Mott's HISTORY OF AMERICAN MAGAZINES.

_____. A HISTORY OF AMERICAN MAGAZINES. 5 vols. Cambridge, Mass.: Harvard University Press, 1957.

The first four volumes of this thorough study cover the years from 1741 to 1905, and include bibliographical facts as well as information on the policies and economics of various periodicals. The following literary magazines are covered in separate chapters. Vol. I (1741-1850): GRAHAM'S, THE WESTERN MONTHLY REVIEW, THE SOUTHERN REVIEW, GODEY'S, THE NEW ENGLAND MAGAZINE, THE AMERICAN MONTHLY REVIEW, THE KNICKERBOCKER MAGAZINE, THE SELECT JOURNAL OF FOREIGN PERIODICAL LITERATURE, THE AMERICAN MONTHLY MAGAZINE, THE LITERARY AND THEOLOGICAL REVIEW, Snowden's LADIES' COMPANION, THE SOUTHERN LITERARY MESSENGER, THE WESTERN MESSENGER, THE SOUTHERN LITERARY JOURNAL, THE LADIES' GARLAND, BURTON'S GENTLEMAN'S MAGAZINE, the DEMOCRATIC REVIEW, THE HESPERIAN, THE MAGNOLIA, the Boston DIAL, the ARCTURUS, MERRY'S MUSEUM, THE BOSTON MISCELLANY, THE SOUTHERN QUARTERLY REVIEW, MISS LESLIE'S MAGAZINE, ARTHUR'S LADIES' MAGAZINE, THE PIONEER, THE COLUMBIAN LADY'S AND GENTLEMAN'S MAGAZINE, LITTELL'S LIVING AGE, THE AMERICAN WHIG REVIEW, THE SOUTHERN AND WESTERN MAGAZINE, THE BROADWAY JOURNAL, THE HARBINGER, Duyckinck's LITERARY WORLD, THE UNION MAGAZINE, THE MASSACHUSETTS QUARTERLY REVIEW, THE JOHN-DONKEY. Vol. II (1850-1865): THE NORTH AMERICAN REVIEW, THE YOUTH'S COMPANION, THE LADIES' REPOSITORY, PETERSON'S MAGAZINE, THE HOME JOURNAL, THE NEW YORK LEDGER, HARPER'S MONTHLY, PUTNAM'S MONTHLY, RUSSELL'S, the ATLANTIC, VANITY FAIR, the Cincinnati DIAL. Vol. III (1865-1885): THE ROUND TABLE, EVERY SATURDAY, THE GALAXY, LIPPINCOTT'S, THE OVERLAND MONTHLY, THE LAKESIDE MONTHLY, OLD AND NEW, PUNCHINELLO, the Boston LITERARY WORLD, SCRIBNER'S-CENTURY, ST. NICHOLAS, PUCK, the Chicago DIAL, THE CRITIC, THE CONTINENT. Vol. IV (1895-1905): THE ARENA, THE CHAP-BOOK, COSMOPOLITAN, CURRENT LITERATURE, LIFE, THE PHILISTINE, THE ROLLING STONE, SCRIBNER'S MAGAZINE.

_____. "Iowa Magazines." PALIMPSEST, 44 (1963), 285-380.

Included in this general survey is a section on "College Literary Magazines" (pp. 303-10), some of them published in the nineteenth century.

_____. "The Magazine Revolution and Popular Ideas in the Nineties." PRO-

CEEDINGS OF THE AMERICAN ANTIQUARIAN SOCIETY, 64 (1954), 195-214.

> The rise of the cheap magazines in the 1890's, including MC-CLURE'S, MUNSEY'S, and COSMOPOLITAN, upset the magazine world and the security of such journals as the ATLANTIC, HARPER'S MONTHLY, and the CENTURY. Mott discusses how these new periodicals reflected the culture of the 1890's in their theme of individual self-improvement, their concern for the "Interests of the Young Man," their support for social reform, and their development of national advertising.

Mueller, Roger Chester. "The Orient in American Transcendental Periodicals (1835-1886)." Dissertation, University of Minnesota, 1968.

> Attitudes toward the Orient and the appearance of Oriental literature in the following periodicals are discussed: THE WESTERN MESSENGER, THE DIAL, THE HARBINGER, THE SPIRIT OF THE AGE, THE MASSACHUSETTS QUARTERLY REVIEW, the Cincinnati DIAL, THE RADICAL, and THE INDEX.

_____. "Transcendental Periodicals and the Orient." EMERSON SOCIETY QUARTERLY, 57 (1969), 52-57.

> THE DIAL and later periodicals such as THE INDEX and THE RADICAL reflect a growing interest in Oriental ideas by the Transcendentalists.

Nelson, Henry Loomis. "American Periodicals." THE DIAL, 28 (1900), 349-52.

> In concluding his brief survey of periodicals from 1880 to 1900, Loomis finds "a notable development of the journals and magazines not wholly devoted to practical questions, to more and higher literary and art criticism, and to perhaps richer expressions of idealism."

Noel, Mary. "The Heyday of the Popular Story Weekly." Dissertation, Columbia University, 1952.

_____. VILLAINS GALORE...THE HEYDAY OF THE POPULAR STORY WEEKLY. New York: Macmillan, 1954.

> These weeklies, also known as mammoths, provided formulized fiction in the cheapest possible format throughout the second half of the nineteenth century. Noel covers the field exhaustively in her study.

North, S.N.D. "History and Present Condition of the Newspaper and Periodical Press of the United States, With a Catalogue of the Publications of the Census Year." REPORT OF THE TENTH CENSUS, 1880. Washington: Government Printing Office, 1884. VIII, i-vi, 1-446.

This report gives a history of newspapers and periodicals in three periods, 1639 to 1783, 1783 to 1835, and 1835 to 1880. Following this are two extensive appendices giving "Statistical Tables" and a "Catalogue of Periodical Publications." North's study presents an exhaustive statistical portrait of the periodical publishing industry.

Northup, Clark Sutherland. "The Periodicals." A MANUAL OF AMERICAN LITERATURE. Ed. Theodore Stanton. New York: G.P. Putnam's Sons, 1909. Pp. 434-54.

This chapter very briefly surveys the important literary periodicals of the eighteenth and nineteenth centuries.

Norton, Charles Eliot. LETTERS OF CHARLES ELIOT NORTON WITH BIO-GRAPHICAL COMMENT BY HIS DAUGHTER SARA NORTON AND M.A. DEWOLFE HOWE. 2 vols. Boston: Houghton, Mifflin, 1913.

Norton gives his views of the ATLANTIC and THE NORTH AMERI-CAN REVIEW, among other periodicals, in his letters.

"An Old-Fashioned Reader's Likes." LITERARY DIGEST, 47 (1913), 285.

The modern journals are deplored and the earlier ones, cheaper paper, poorer illustrations, drab covers and all, are preferred for their contents.

Orians, G. Harrison. "Censure of Fiction in American Romances and Magazines, 1789-1810." PMLA, 52 (1937), 195-214.

"Although there was little abatement of active opposition before the War of 1812, yet critics of the time, dismayed over the futility of their abuse, speedily sought hope in fatherly guidance."

Palfrey, J.G. "Periodical Literature of the United States." THE NORTH AMERICAN REVIEW, 39 (1834), 277-301.

The editor of THE NORTH AMERICAN REVIEW recounts in detail the history of some literary periodicals as well as newspapers up to his time, and in the process makes some interesting observations, especially considering his perspective.

Pattee, Fred Lewis. THE DEVELOPMENT OF THE AMERICAN SHORT STORY: AN HISTORICAL SURVEY. New York: Harper and Brothers, 1923.

Pattee says quite a bit about the literary periodicals as he examines the history of the short story. Most significant is Chapter IV on "The Rise of the Lady's Books" (pp. 69-90). He sees the founding of the ATLANTIC as an important reaction against the sentimentality of lady's book literature, and later THE NATION'S emphasis on objective, scientific criticism as an accompaniment to the realistic movement in American fiction.

Pecek, Louis George. "The Beadle Story Papers, 1870-1897: A Study of Popular Fiction." Dissertation, Ohio State University, 1959.

> The contents of the three following story papers published by the firm of Beadle and Adams are analyzed: the SATURDAY JOURNAL (1870-1882), BEADLE'S WEEKLY (1882-1885), and THE BANNER WEEKLY (1885-1897).

"The Periodical Literature of America." BLACKWOOD'S EDINBURGH MAGAZINE, 63 (1848), 106-12.

> "In examining the causes of the inferiority of American periodical literature, the most readily assignable, and generally applicable, is that its contributors are mostly unpaid. It is pretty safe to enunciate as a general rule, that, when you want a good thing, you must pay for it."

Perry, Bliss. "Literary Criticism in American Periodicals." THE PRAISE OF FOLLY AND OTHER PAPERS. Port Washington, N.Y.: Kennikat Press, 1964. Pp. 171-231. First printed in YALE REVIEW, NS 3 (1914), 635-55.

> Perry examines the search for an adequate standard for literary criticism by American editors, from Joseph Dennie and Edgar Allan Poe onward. He concludes that modern criticism is often inadequate.

Repplier, Agnes. "American Magazines." YALE REVIEW, 16 (1927), 261-74.

> The essayist reminisces about nineteenth-century periodicals, including THE KNICKERBOCKER and GRAHAM'S, which lined the bookshelves at home when she was a child.

Reynolds, Quentin. THE FICTION FACTORY OR FROM PULP ROW TO QUALITY STREET. New York: Random House, 1955

> This history of the Street & Smith publishing firm discusses various of its story papers and all-fiction periodicals.

Robbins, J. Albert. "Fees Paid to Authors by Certain American Periodicals, 1840-1850." STUDIES IN BIBLIOGRAPHY, 2 (1949-50), 95-104.

> Robbins concludes from his study that "contributing to magazines could afford a convenient supplement to one's income, but as a sole source of income it was obviously insufficient."

_____. "Mrs. Emma C. Embury's Account Book: A Study of Some of her Periodical Contributions." BULLETIN OF THE NEW YORK PUBLIC LIBRARY, 51 (1947), 479-85.

> The financial record of Mrs. Embury's contributions of sentimental literature in the late 1830's and the 1840's "sheds some light on the relationship of author and magazine publisher in a time when

there were few writers who did not seek a larger audience of
readers through periodical publication."

Schramm, Richard Howard. "The Image of India in Selected American Literary
Periodicals: 1870-1900." Dissertation, Duke University, 1964.

The views of India in the poetry, fiction, and non-fiction of a
number of periodicals are analyzed.

Scudder, Horace Elisha. JAMES RUSSELL LOWELL: A BIOGRAPHY. 2 vols.
Boston: Houghton, Mifflin, 1901.

Lowell edited THE PIONEER, the ATLANTIC, and THE NORTH
AMERICAN REVIEW, and contributed to other literary periodicals
throughout his career.

Siegel, Gerald. "The Poe-esque Tale in American Magazines, 1830-1860."
Dissertation, George Washington University, 1972.

After ascertaining the elements of the Poe-esque tale, Siegel investigates the prevalence of the form in the magazines. He finds it
to be less popular than the "domestic-sentimental" and "adventure-
romance" varieties.

Simpson, Lewis P. "'The Literary Miscellany' and 'The General Repository':
Two Cambridge Periodicals of the Early Republic." LIBRARY CHRONICLE OF
THE UNIVERSITY OF TEXAS, 3 (1950), 177-90.

Simpson investigates the editing and publishing history of these two
periodicals founded early in the nineteenth century. He considers
them important, though short-lived, predecessors of THE NORTH
AMERICAN REVIEW, because they, along with THE MONTHLY
ANTHOLOGY, laid the groundwork for the success of the later
journal.

_____. THE MAN OF LETTERS IN NEW ENGLAND AND THE SOUTH: ES-
SAYS ON THE HISTORY OF THE LITERARY VOCATION IN AMERICA. Baton
Rouge: Louisiana State University Press, 1973.

Among these essays are two which investigate the careers and ideas
of men associated with THE MONTHLY ANTHOLOGY, Joseph Ste-
vens Buckminster and William Tudor. A piece on "Poe's Vision of
His Ideal Magazine" (pp. 131-49) is included with the essays on
southern literary ideas.

Spencer, Benjamin T. "A National Literature, 1837-1855." AMERICAN LIT-
ERATURE, 8 (1936), 125-59.

This article shows the drive for a national literature led by men
like Emerson and E.P. Whipple, and the adverse reaction by Longfellow, Lowell, and others. Since he relies on them for much of

his evidence, Spencer reveals how this issue was reflected in the
literary journals of the period.

_____. THE QUEST FOR NATIONALITY: AN AMERICAN LITERARY CAM-
PAIGN. Syracuse: Syracuse University Press, 1957.

American literary nationalism found expression naturally in the
periodicals, and Spencer reveals much about them in the course of
his discussion.

Sprague, Julian K. "Jumping Frog and N.Y. SATURDAY PRESS--Boston and
the N.Y. Bohemians--W.D. Howells and 'Literary Friends.'" TWAINIAN,
18 (March-April 1959), 1-4.

Howells' accounts in LITERARY FRIENDS AND ACQUAINTANCE of
his work on THE SATURDAY PRESS and the ATLANTIC are quoted
and discussed. His work on these periodicals was important to Mark
Twain, who contributed to both journals.

Stearns, Bertha M. "Before GODEY'S." AMERICAN LITERATURE, 2 (1930),
248-55.

This article provides information on some of the many ladies' literary magazines which preceded GODEY'S, "to suggest what they
were like, and to call attention to the influence they may have
had in providing later writers with an audience."

_____. "John Howard Payne as an Editor." AMERICAN LITERATURE, 5
(1933), 215-28.

Among Payne's activities was an abortive attempt to found a literary
periodical for England and America to be published in London.

Strohecker, Edwin Charles. "American Juvenile Literary Periodicals, 1789-
1826." Dissertation, University of Michigan, 1969.

Twenty-five magazines are examined for general trends during the
period.

Tassin, Algernon. THE MAGAZINE IN AMERICA. New York: Dodd, Mead,
1916. First published in THE BOOKMAN, 40 (1915), 659-73; 41 (1915), 138-
51, 284-96, 369-80, 521-33, 620-32; 42 (1915-1916), 59-72, 135-47, 288-
301, 396-412.

Tassin's book examines the literary journal from its beginnings in
the eighteenth century through its development to 1900. Although
he provides neither footnotes nor a formal bibliography, and his
writing style is at times overly witty and contorted, he does include
a vast amount of bibliographical detail about periodicals from all
sections of the country.

Tebbel, John. THE AMERICAN MAGAZINE: A COMPACT HISTORY. New York: Hawthorn, 1969.

> This one-volume history covers the field from the earliest colonial magazines through those of the twentieth century, and although not focusing on them exclusively, it includes information on many literary periodicals. This work is aimed at the general reader, and contains no footnotes or extensive bibliography.

Thomas, Isaiah. THE HISTORY OF PRINTING IN AMERICA, WITH A BIBLIOGRAPHY OF PRINTERS, AND AN ACCOUNT OF NEWSPAPERS. 2nd ed. 2 vols. Transactions and Collections of the American Antiquarian Society, vols. 5 and 6. Albany: Joel Munsell, 1874.

> Volume II presents histories of newspapers and journals from various states that were published before the Revolution. Also, an appendix on pp. 292-93 lists "Magazines and Other Periodical Works Published in the United States in 1810."

Towne, Charles Hanson. "The One-Man Magazines." THE AMERICAN MERCURY, 63 (1946), 104-8.

> Towne maintains that often the most successful magazines are those run by one man, and in this connection he discusses Reedy of REEDY'S MIRROR, Stone of THE CHAP-BOOK, Burgess of THE LARK, and others, most, like the last two, creators of little magazines in the 1890's.

Vanderbilt, Kermit. CHARLES ELIOT NORTON: APOSTLE OF CULTURE IN A DEMOCRACY. Cambridge: Belknap Press of Harvard University Press, 1959.

> Chapter III, "The Journalist and Civil War Optimism," covers the period from 1857 to 1867 when "Norton exerted all the energies of his mind and heart to the shaping of public character and popular opinion, first as a writer for the ATLANTIC and editor for the Loyal Publication Society; then as co-editor (with Lowell) of THE NORTH AMERICAN REVIEW during and after the war; and finally as a founder of THE NATION."

Voorhees, Oscar M. THE HISTORY OF PHI BETA KAPPA. New York: Crown Publishers, 1945.

> A section on "Early Phi Beta Kappa Periodicals" (pp. 93-99) discusses the founding of literary journals at Yale, Harvard, Dartmouth, and in New York by various chapters or individual members of the fraternity.

Wagner, Frederick. "Travel Writing About the British Isles and France in Selected American Literary Periodicals, 1865-1890." Dissertation, Duke University, 1971.

> Wagner analyzes the travel literature found in the following period-

icals: the ATLANTIC, HARPER'S MONTHLY, SCRIBNER'S MONTH-
LY, and the CENTURY.

Weeks, Lewis Ernest, Jr. "American and British Periodical Criticism of Certain
Nineteenth-Century American Authors, 1840-1860." Dissertation, Boston University, 1961.

> Critical views in about a dozen American periodicals are compared
> to those in the same number of British publications. Generally, and
> surprisingly, these views are found to be in agreement.

Wood, James Playsted. MAGAZINES IN THE UNITED STATES: THEIR SOCIAL
AND ECONOMIC INFLUENCE. 2nd ed. New York: Ronald Press, 1956.

> Although this is a history of American magazines generally from
> colonial days to the present, Wood discusses literary journals in
> Chapter III, "Magazines as National Educators: THE PORT FOLIO
> and Its Contemporaries," and Chapter IV, "Early General Maga-
> zines as a Literary Force."

Woodall, Guy R. "Robert Walsh, Jr., as an Editor and Literary Critic: 1797-
1836." Dissertation, University of Tennessee, 1966.

> Woodall examines Walsh's career as a literary critic and editor of
> various periodicals, and discusses Walsh's opinions about the litera-
> ture of his period.

Woodberry, George E. "Lowell's Letters to Poe." SCRIBNER'S MAGAZINE,
16 (1894), 170-76.

> Two main subjects of these letters are Poe's contributions to and
> Lowell's struggle with THE PIONEER, and Poe's projected but un-
> realized STYLUS literary journal.

Ziff, Larzer. THE AMERICAN 1890's: LIFE AND TIMES OF A LOST GEN-
ERATION. New York: Viking Press, 1966.

> In Chapter VI, "The Tinkle of the Little Bell: Magazines," Ziff
> investigates the rise of the cheap magazines such as MCCLURE'S
> and the little magazines such as THE CHAP-BOOK, and he also
> examines the policies of the quality journals, the ATLANTIC, the
> CENTURY, and HARPER'S MONTHLY.

Chapter 3

LITERARY PERIODICALS OF NEW ENGLAND

Chapter 3

LITERARY PERIODICALS OF NEW ENGLAND

General Studies

Beatty, Richard Croom. JAMES RUSSELL LOWELL. Nashville: Vanderbilt University Press, 1942.

> The short history of Lowell's PIONEER is covered on pp. 46–49, and the founding of the ATLANTIC and Lowell's involvement with that periodical are discussed on pp. 144–65.

Cooke, George Willis. UNITARIANISM IN AMERICA: A HISTORY OF ITS ORIGIN AND DEVELOPMENT. Boston: American Unitarian Association, 1910.

> Chapter V, "The Period of Controversy," touches upon the following more or less literary periodicals: THE MONTHLY ANTHOLOGY, THE GENERAL REPOSITORY AND REVIEW, THE CHRISTIAN DISCIPLE, and THE NORTH AMERICAN REVIEW.

Cummings, Charles A. "Chapter XX. The Press and Literature of the Last Hundred Years." THE MEMORIAL HISTORY OF BOSTON, INCLUDING SUFFOLK COUNTY. 1630-1880. Ed. Justin Winsor. Boston: James R. Osgood, 1881. III, 617-82.

> This study includes material on all of the major literary periodicals from THE MASSACHUSETTS MAGAZINE to the ATLANTIC.

Gohdes, Clarence L. THE PERIODICALS OF AMERICAN TRANSCENDENTALISM. Durham, N.C.: Duke University Press, 1931.

> Gohdes studies in detail the periodicals, except for THE DIAL, produced by various individuals in the Transcendental movement. He focuses on the philosophical content of the journals. Chapters are devoted to THE WESTERN MESSENGER, THE BOSTON QUARTERLY REVIEW, THE PRESENT, THE HARBINGER, THE SPIRIT OF THE AGE, the AESTHETIC PAPERS, THE MASSACHUSETTS QUARTERLY REVIEW, the Cincinnati DIAL, THE RADICAL, and THE INDEX.

Hale, Edward Everett. JAMES RUSSELL LOWELL AND HIS FRIENDS. Boston: Houghton, Mifflin, 1899.

> Chapter X, "Lowell's Experience as an Editor," deals with Lowell's editorship of the ATLANTIC and THE NORTH AMERICAN REVIEW. Pp. 82-86 discuss Nathan Hale, Jr.'s BOSTON MISCELLANY OF LITERATURE AND FASHION.

Higginson, Thomas Wentworth. "Old Cambridge in Three Literary Epochs." OLD CAMBRIDGE. New York: Macmillan, 1900. Pp. 41-71.

> Higginson establishes the dates of each epoch according to the initial publication of first THE NORTH AMERICAN REVIEW (1815), then THE DIAL (1840), and finally the ATLANTIC (1857). He also publishes letters he received from Francis H. Underwood in 1853 concerning plans which four years later resulted in the AT-LANTIC's appearance.

Lowell, James Russell. LETTERS OF JAMES RUSSELL LOWELL. 2 vols. New York: Harper and Brothers, 1894.

> Lowell refers in his letters to his editorship of the ATLANTIC, THE NORTH AMERICAN REVIEW, and THE PIONEER, and he comments on other periodicals, as in his letter to C.F. Briggs in 1845 about THE BROADWAY JOURNAL.

_____. NEW LETTERS OF JAMES RUSSELL LOWELL. Ed. M.A. DeWolfe Howe. New York: Harper and Brothers, 1932.

> Many of the letters in the section "Editor and Teacher, 1857-1877" (pp. 92-225) involve Lowell's editorship of the ATLANTIC.

Norton, Charles Eliot. LETTERS OF CHARLES ELIOT NORTON. Eds. Sarah Norton and M.A. DeWolfe Howe. 2 vols. Boston: Houghton, Mifflin, 1913.

> In some of his letters Norton discusses the policies of the ATLAN-TIC, and in others THE NORTH AMERICAN REVIEW, which he edited along with Lowell.

Rabinovitz, Albert L. "Criticism of French Novels in Boston Magazines: 1830-1860." NEW ENGLAND QUARTERLY, 14 (1941), 488-504.

> Although some editors, such as Margaret Fuller and Orestes Brownson, published more works by French novelists than others such as Francis Bowen, generally the views held in Boston magazines were more liberal than those expressed in other parts of the country.

Smart, George K. "A Note on THE PERIODICALS OF AMERICAN TRANSCEN-DENTALISM." AMERICAN LITERATURE, 10 (1939), 494-95.

> Smart corrects a misstatement made in Gohdes' book concerning Orestes Brownson.

Stearns, Bertha M. "Early Factory Magazines in New England: The LOWELL OFFERING and Its Contemporaries." JOURNAL OF ECONOMIC AND BUSINESS HISTORY, 2 (1930), 685-705.

> Stearns presents bibliographical information and a discussion of the contents of a number of literary periodicals published by factory girls throughout New England in the 1840's.

_____. "Early New England Magazines for Ladies." NEW ENGLAND QUARTERLY, 2 (1929), 429-57.

> Various literary journals of the nineteenth century published specifically for women are examined, concluding with a discussion of Mrs. Sarah Josepha Hale's LADIES' MAGAZINE and her subsequent move to edit GODEY'S LADY'S BOOK.

_____. "New England Magazines for Ladies, 1830-1860." NEW ENGLAND QUARTERLY, 3 (1930), 627-56.

> "From 1830 to 1860 [New England] provided no fewer than thirty such periodicals, all of them offering a welcome to the literary efforts of women, and many of them presided over by women editors." The article includes bibliographical information and discusses the contents of these magazines.

Studies of Individual Periodicals

AESTHETIC PAPERS (1849)

Jones, Joseph. "Introduction." AESTHETIC PAPERS (1849). Ed. Elizabeth P. Peabody. 1849; rpt. Gainesville, Fla.: Scholars' Facsimiles & Reprints, 1957. Pp. i-xii.

> In an introduction to this reprint of the periodical's one and only issue, Jones supplies information about contributors, contemporary literary journals of the Transcendentalist movement, and the goals of the editor.

_____. "Villages as Universities: AESTHETIC PAPERS and a Passage in WALDEN." EMERSON SOCIETY QUARTERLY, 7 (II Quarter 1957), 40-42.

> Similar passages in WALDEN and an article by Elizabeth Peabody in her periodical show either that Thoreau was influenced by the AESTHETIC PAPERS article or else the two Transcendentalists shared a common outside source of influence.

* * * * *

ATLANTIC MONTHLY (1857-current)

Austin, James C. FIELDS OF THE ATLANTIC MONTHLY: LETTERS TO AN

EDITOR, 1861-1870. San Marino, Calif.: Huntington Library, 1953.

> This collection explores Fields' editorship through his correspondence, and in addition gives background on those to whom he wrote, including their relationship to the magazine.

Baker, Portia. "Walt Whitman and the ATLANTIC MONTHLY." AMERICAN LITERATURE, 6 (1934), 283-301.

> True to its conservative outlook, the ATLANTIC either ignored or coolly received Whitman's poetry throughout his career, and only in his later years did its opinions soften at all toward him.

Baldwin, Lida F. "Unbound Old ATLANTICS." ATLANTIC, 100 (1907), 679-89.

> Baldwin tells of her childhood pleasure in reading the stories and poems found in old ATLANTICS stashed in her father's desk drawer.

Bandy, W.T. "James Russell Lowell, Sainte-Beuve, and the ATLANTIC MONTHLY." COMPARATIVE LITERATURE, 11 (1959), 229-32.

> Sainte-Beuve contributed an article to the magazine in 1858 which editor Lowell translated.

Bernard, Edward G. "New Light on Lowell as Editor." NEW ENGLAND QUARTERLY, 10 (1937), 337-41.

> Letters written to Parke Godwin reveal the extensive influence Lowell had on contributors to the magazine, as well as his own interest in political articles.

Birss, John H. "Herman Melville and the ATLANTIC MONTHLY." NOTES AND QUERIES, 167 (1934), 223-24.

> A letter dated August 19, 1857, is here reprinted in which Melville promises Francis H. Underwood that he will contribute to the ATLANTIC. He never did fulfill the promise.

Brawley, Agnes B. "Attitudes Toward Realism and Science in the ATLANTIC MONTHLY, 1880-1900." Dissertation, University of Wisconsin, 1954.

Brill, Leonard. "Thomas Wentworth Higginson and the ATLANTIC MONTHLY." Dissertation, University of Minnesota, 1968.

> Brill examines Higginson's association with the magazine throughout its first fifty years.

Brooks, Van Wyck. HOWELLS: HIS LIFE AND WORLD. New York: E.P. Dutton, 1959.

> Howell's editing of the ATLANTIC from 1872 to 1881, and his policy of opening its pages to literature from all sections of the country, are discussed in Chapter VIII, "Editor and Playwright."

Budd, Louis, J. "Howells, The ATLANTIC MONTHLY, and Republicanism."

AMERICAN LITERATURE, 24 (1952), 139-56.

> The main thrust of this essay is that "during his ten years editing the ATLANTIC Howells was a political journalist as well as a literary critic, that he aided the Republican party from Boston just as he had done from Columbus and New York City, that he made the ATLANTIC reflect political views acceptable to himself and most educated Republicans, and that he in the main allowed his magazine to voice the conservative rationale."

Butler, Robert E. "William Dean Howells as Editor of the ATLANTIC MONTHLY." Dissertation, Rutgers University, 1950.

Downey, Jean. "ATLANTIC Friends: Howells and Cooke." AMERICAN NOTES & QUERIES, 1 (1963), 132-33.

> Correspondence reveals Rose Terry Cooke's relationship with the ATLANTIC as a contributor during the editorships of Howells, Thomas Bailey Aldrich, and finally Horace Scudder.

Duberman, Martin. JAMES RUSSELL LOWELL. Boston: Houghton, Mifflin, 1966.

> Chapter VIII entitled "Professor and Editor" covers the founding of the ATLANTIC and investigates in detail Lowell's policies as the first editor. His work on THE PIONEER and THE NORTH AMERICAN REVIEW is also discussed in this study.

Emerson, Edward Waldo. THE EARLY YEARS OF THE SATURDAY CLUB. Boston: Houghton, Mifflin, 1918.

> Chapter II covers the establishment of the Atlantic, or Magazine, Club and the subsequent founding of the periodical.

"Forty Years of the ATLANTIC MONTHLY." ATLANTIC, 80 (1897), 571-76.

> This sketch of the journal's history relates some interesting details, such as the adverse reaction of some religious periodicals to the ATLANTIC's publication of Oliver Wendell Holmes' AUTOCRAT OF THE BREAKFAST-TABLE. The contemporary contents of the journal are compared favorably to those of earlier years.

Gilman, Arthur. "ATLANTIC Dinners and Diners." ATLANTIC, 100 (1907), 646-57.

> Gilman relates anecdotes and quotes poetry from dinners he attended with ATLANTIC contributors and editors.

_____. "The Contributor's Club." ATLANTIC, 100 (1907), 715-20.

> Gilman reminisces about his work for ATLANTIC editor James T. Fields.

Gohdes, Clarence. "The ATLANTIC Celebrates Its Hundredth Birthday." SOUTH ATLANTIC QUARTERLY, 57 (1958), 163-67.

Gohdes reiterates the story of the founding of the ATLANTIC and conjectures about the magazine's great success.

Hendrick, Burton J. THE LIFE AND LETTERS OF WALTER H. PAGE. 3 vols. Garden City, N.Y.: Doubleday, Page and Co., 1923.

Pp. 53-63 of Volume I cover Page's editorship of the ATLANTIC and include an account by Ellery Sedgwick, a later ATLANTIC editor, of the "somewhat disconcerting descent of Page upon the editorial sanctuary of James Russell Lowell."

Higginson, Thomas Wentworth. CHEERFUL YESTERDAYS. Boston: Houghton, Mifflin, 1898.

Higginson remembers the ATLANTIC's founding, the famous dinners, and Fields and Lowell as editors in Chapter VI, "The Birth of a Literature." The chapter's title indicates the importance he places upon the journal's role in American literary history.

_____. LETTERS AND JOURNALS OF THOMAS WENTWORTH HIGGINSON: 1846-1906. Ed. Mary Thacher Higginson. New York: Negro Universities Press, 1921.

On pp. 107-14 Higginson discusses his experiences at the ATLAN-TIC dinners and also complains about the journal's weak stand against slavery at the outbreak of the Civil War.

Hough, Robert L. THE QUIET REBEL: WILLIAM DEAN HOWELS AS SOCIAL COMMENTATOR. Lincoln: University of Nebraska Press, 1959.

Chapter III on "Howells and the ATLANTIC" demonstrates that after his ten-year experience as editor, "it seems fair to say that in 1881 the love for the old America was still strong in Howells, but like others, he was beginning to see that the new reality was different from the earlier dreams." The ATLANTIC's contents during this time reflected Howells' feelings.

Howe, M.A. DeWolfe. THE ATLANTIC MONTHLY AND ITS MAKERS. Boston: Atlantic Monthly Press, 1919.

The journal's history is traced through the reigns of its successive editors, and Howe amply supplies his narrative with anecdotes.

Howells, William Dean. "Recollections of an ATLANTIC Editorship." ATLAN-TIC, 100 (1907), 594-606.

The former editor remembers his feelings when he accepted or rejected a manuscript, his sense of relief and then regret when he left the position, and other impressions from this period in his career.

Hudson, Randolph. "ATLANTIC MONTHLY Authorship, 1857-1861." AMERI-CAN NOTES & QUERIES, 3 (1964-65), 6-7, 22-23, 36-37, 56-57, 69-70, 86-87, 102-3, 118-19, 133-34.

During this period the magazine published all of its work anonymously, and the identities of the authors of these contributions are here supplied.

JUBILEE: ONE HUNDRED YEARS OF THE ATLANTIC. Eds. Edward Weeks and Emily Flint. Boston: Little, Brown, 1957.

This anthology gives a good selection of the magazine's contents, and thus its tone and policies, throughout its history. Short introductions to each section also present valuable background information.

Kirk, Clara M. and Rudolf. WILLIAM DEAN HOWELLS. New York: Twayne, 1962.

Chapter II on Howells as "Editor and Novelist" presents details of his work first as an assistant editor and then as editor of the ATLANTIC. Chapter V, "Novelist in the 'Easy Chair,'" discusses his work as contributing editor for HARPER'S MONTHLY.

Lynn, Kenneth S. WILLIAM DEAN HOWELLS: AN AMERICAN LIFE. New York: Harcourt Brace Javonovich, 1971.

Chapter VIII, "An Editor and His Friends," gives excerpts from Howells' frank book reviews written before he became the ATLANTIC's editor, and then examines his editorship, its policies, and the personal contacts he made during those years.

McMahon, Helen. CRITICISM OF FICTION: A STUDY OF TRENDS IN THE ATLANTIC MONTHLY, 1857-1898. New York: Bookman Associates, 1952.

The ATLANTIC's support for and theories concerning realistic fiction are revealed in the critical writings of Howells, Henry James, Bliss Perry, George Lathrop, and Horace Scudder. A "Register of Reviews and Critical Essays" (pp. 137-79) is also included. This study is based on a dissertation completed at the University of Iowa in 1952.

Mitchell, Robert E. "American Life as Reflected in the ATLANTIC MONTHLY, 1857-1881." Dissertation, Harvard University, 1951.

Morse, John T. LIFE AND LETTERS OF OLIVER WENDELL HOLMES. 2 vols. London: Sampson Low, Marston, 1896.

The ATLANTIC's founding, Holmes' role in naming it, and his contributions to it are all covered here.

"Mr. Scudder and the ATLANTIC." ATLANTIC, 89 (1902), 433-34.

Scudder's relationship with the ATLANTIC is briefly reviewed.

Norton, Charles Eliot. "The Launching of the Magazine." ATLANTIC, 100 (1907), 579-81.

Norton recounts his personal involvement in the journal's founding and regrets the decline in the quality of American literature which he feels has occurred since.

Perry, Bliss. "The Arlington Street Incarnation." ATLANTIC, 150 (1932), 515-18.

The sole surviving ex-editor reminisces about the journal's past. This anniversary number reprints some contributions from throughout the ATLANTIC's history.

_____. "The Editor Who Was Never an Editor." PARK-STREET PAPERS. Boston: Houghton, Mifflin, 1908. Pp. 203-77.

This is an interesting piece about Francis H. Underwood, a founder of the ATLANTIC who worked hard for its success but never received much recognition. Perry quotes extensively from Underwood's file of letters in order to "throw light upon the unwritten history of the ATLANTIC...."

Schweik, Robert C. "The 'Duplicate' Manuscript of Hardy's 'Two on a Tower': A Correction and a Comment." PAPERS OF THE BIBLIOGRAPHICAL SOCIETY OF AMERICA, 60 (1966), 219-21.

Schweik discusses the possibility that two manuscripts of TWO ON A TOWER were involved in the editing of the work for publication in the ATLANTIC, a theory put forth by Carl J. Weber in his article in the PAPERS, 40 (1946), 1-21.

Scudder, Horace. THE ATLANTIC INDEX and ATLANTIC INDEX SUPPLEMENT. 1903; rpt. Washington, D.C.: Carrollton Press, n.d.

This is a list of authors and articles for the volumes up to 1901.

Ticknor, Caroline. HAWTHORNE AND HIS PUBLISHER. Boston: Houghton, Mifflin, 1913.

Chapter XVI, "The ATLANTIC MONTHLY," sketches the publishing and editing history, and ends with a comment on Hawthorne's late contributions.

Trowbridge, John Townsend. "An Early Contributor's Recollections." ATLANTIC, 100 (1907), 582-93.

Trowbridge recalls the journal's early days, extensively discussing Brownell, the poet and contributor to the ATLANTIC who Trowbridge feels has been undeservedly ignored.

_____. "The Author of Quabbin." ATLANTIC, 75 (1895), 108-16.

In yet another reminiscence the writer recalls his long friendship with Francis H. Underwood, and reiterates Underwood's role in founding the ATLANTIC. Other people associated with the periodical in its early years are also discussed.

_____. MY OWN STORY: WITH RECOLLECTIONS OF NOTED PERSONS.
Boston: Houghton, Mifflin, 1903.

> Chapter VII on "Underwood, Lowell, and THE ATLANTIC MONTH-
> LY" covers the journal's initiation and Trowbridge's personal involve-
> ment as a contributor.

Tryon, W.S. PARNASSUS CORNER: A LIFE OF JAMES T. FIELDS, PUBLISH-
ER TO THE VICTORIANS. Boston: Houghton, Mifflin, 1963.

> Chapter XII, "War and the Editorship of the ATLANTIC: 1860-
> 1865," examines the different versions of how Ticknor and Fields
> obtained the ATLANTIC, and then relates in detail Fields' policies
> as editor and some anecdotes about his association with the maga-
> zine's contributors.

Weber, Carl J. "The Manuscript of Hardy's TWO ON A TOWER." PAPERS
OF THE BIBLIOGRAPHICAL SOCIETY OF AMERICA, 40 (1942), 1-21.

> Editor Thomas Bailey Aldrich altered Hardy's novel before serializing
> it in the ATLANTIC.

Woodress, James L., Jr. "Comfort Me, O My Publisher: Some Unpublished
Letters from James Russell Lowell to James T. Fields." HUNTINGTON LIBRA-
RY QUARTERLY, 15 (1951), 73-86.

> These letters were written between 1863 and 1869, when Fields was
> a partner in his book-publishing firm and the editor of the ATLAN-
> TIC as well. His relationship with Lowell involved both positions,
> for he solicited the writer's journalistic contributions and published
> his books.

*   *   *   *   *

THE BOSTON NOTION (1841-1844)

Pollin, Burton R. "Poe and the BOSTON NOTION." ENGLISH LANGUAGE
NOTES, 8 (1970), 23-28.

> Pollin examines "the treatment accorded Poe by this one of the
> more significant Boston publications, unfortunately now rare and
> almost unavailable."

_____. "Poe in the BOSTON NOTION." NEW ENGLAND QUARTERLY, 42
(1969), 585-89.

> Poe's relationship with Robert Carter, editor of the NOTION, is
> examined.

*   *   *   *   *

THE CHRISTIAN EXAMINER (1818-1869)

Mott, Frank Luther. "THE CHRISTIAN DISCIPLE and THE CHRISTIAN EXAM-
INER." NEW ENGLAND QUARTERLY, 1 (1928), 197-207.

The EXAMINER, which originated as the DISCIPLE (1813-1818), experienced numerous changes in subtitle, place of publication, and editor in its career from 1818 to 1869. Mott traces these changes, including the philosophical one from Unitarianism to Transcendentalism that occurred under Frederick H. Hedge in 1857.

*   *   *   *   *

THE DIAL (1840-1844)

Anderson, Charles R. "Thoreau and THE DIAL: The Apprentice Years." ESSAYS MOSTLY ON PERIODICAL PUBLISHING IN AMERICA. Durham, N.C.: Duke University Press, 1973. Pp. 92-120.

Thoreau submitted some of his early work to THE DIAL while Emerson was editor, including the essay "A Winter Walk" and the poem "Dark Ages," the last quoted in full by Anderson because he feels critics have ignored it. THE DIAL thus served Thoreau as a literary training ground.

Cabot, James Elliot. A MEMOIR OF RALPH WALDO EMERSON. 2 vols. Boston: Houghton, Mifflin, 1887.

Chapter XI covers Emerson's editorship of THE DIAL, emphasizing his growing disappointment with the project. Also included as "Appendix C" is a "List of Mr. Emerson's Contributions to THE DIAL."

Carlyle, Thomas, and Ralph Waldo Emerson. THE CORRESPONDENCE OF EMERSON AND CARLYLE. Ed. Joseph Slater. New York: Columbia University Press, 1964.

Emerson writes of his personal feelings about THE DIAL and his role in its publication, and Carlyle responds with his critical judgment of the journal.

Cary, Elisabeth Luther. EMERSON: POET AND THINKER. New York: G.P. Putnam's Sons, 1904.

Chapter VIII presents biographical information on the people involved in THE DIAL's founding and career, and Chapter IX surveys the journal's contents, especially during the period of Emerson's editorship. An Appendix (pp. 265-79) lists the contents and contributors of THE DIAL, based on information in the studies of Cabot and Cooke (see this section).

Cooke, George Willis. "The DIAL." JOURNAL OF SPECULATIVE PHILOSOPHY, 19 (1885), 225-65.

Cooke traces THE DIAL's complete history, discusses its contents and goals, and offers short biographical sketches of major and minor figures involved with the journal. The tables of contents for all issues are included at the end of the study.

_____. "The DIAL and Corrigenda." JOURNAL OF SPECULATIVE PHILOSO-
PHY, 19 (1885), 322-23.

A few corrections are made to the above study.

_____. AN HISTORICAL AND BIOGRAPHICAL INTRODUCTION TO ACCOM-
PANY THE DIAL AS REPRINTED IN NUMBERS FOR THE ROWFANT CLUB. 2
vols. Cleveland: Rowfant Club, 1902.

In this exhaustive study Cooke not only examines THE DIAL as it
was published under Margaret Fuller and Emerson, but he places
the magazine in its philosophical context. Chapter XII of Volume
II covers "Successors to the DIAL," including THE HARBINGER,
THE MASSACHUSETTS QUARTERLY REVIEW, and the Cincinnati
DIAL.

_____. RALPH WALDO EMERSON: HIS LIFE, WRITINGS, AND PHILOSO-
PHY. 2nd ed. Boston: James R. Osgood, 1882.

Chapter VII on THE DIAL gives a detailed account of Emerson's
work on the magazine, including a reprinting in full of his intro-
ductory article in the first number.

Curtis, George William. "Ralph Waldo Emerson and 'The Dial.'" JOURNAL
OF SPECULATIVE PHILOSOPHY, 16 (1882), 330-31.

Upon notice that the magazine is to be reprinted, Curtis praises
THE DIAL and Emerson's work on it.

Emerson, Ralph Waldo. JOURNALS OF RALPH WALDO EMERSON, WITH AN-
NOTATIONS. Eds. Edward Waldo Emerson and Waldo Emerson Forbes. Boston:
Houghton, Mifflin, 1911.

Volumes V and VI contain a few of Emerson's thoughts on THE DIAL.

Emerson, R.W., W.H. Channing, and J.F. Clarke. MEMOIRS OF MARGARET
FULLER OSSOLI. 2 vols. Boston: Phillips, Sampson, 1852.

Pp. 24-31 cover Margaret Fuller's editorship of THE DIAL, mostly
by quoting long passages from letters she wrote expressing her views
on the journal.

Firkins, O.W. RALPH WALDO EMERSON. Boston: Houghton, Mifflin, 1915.

Firkins expresses some negative criticism of THE DIAL and its group
on pp. 95-101. For one thing its supporters failed to see the ob-
vious reasons for their periodical's lack of popularity.

Frothingham, Octavius Brooks. TRANSCENDENTALISM IN NEW ENGLAND.
New York: Harper and Brothers, 1959.

Pp. 132-35 cover the contents, editors, and important dates in the
history of THE DIAL.

Goddard, Harold Clarke. STUDIES IN NEW ENGLAND TRANSCENDENTAL-

ISM. New York: Hillary House, 1960.

> On pp. 36-38 Goddard quickly surveys the founding of THE DIAL, its reception by the public, and the various attitudes toward it of the magazine's own group.

Gohdes, Clarence. "Alcott's 'Conversation' on the Transcendental Club and THE DIAL." AMERICAN LITERATURE, 3 (1931), 14-27.

> This article reprints in full the "conversation" delivered by Bronson Alcott on March 23, 1863, the first half of which centers on the Transcendentalists generally, and the second half on THE DIAL.

Hennessy, Helen. "The DIAL: Its Poetry and Poetic Criticism." NEW ENGLAND QUARTERLY, 31 (1958), 66-87.

> Although the poetry "has little aesthetic appeal...taken as a body it bears witness to the transcendental movement more concisely and perhaps more arrestingly than the voluminous transcendental production in prose."

Higginson, Thomas Wentworth. MARGARET FULLER OSSOLI. Boston: Houghton, Mifflin, 1884.

> Chapter IX on "A Literary Club and Its Organ" and Chapter X on "The DIAL" cover Margaret Fuller's editorship of the journal, including her correspondence with contributors, her attitude toward her work, and finally the exhaustion that resulted.

Holmes, Oliver Wendell. RALPH WALDO EMERSON. Boston: Houghton, Mifflin, 1884.

> Emerson's opinions about THE DIAL, especially as expressed to Thomas Carlyle, and his activities on the journal, are discussed on pp. 158-63.

Marshall, H.E. "The Story of the DIAL." NEW MEXICO QUARTERLY, 1 (1931), 147-65.

Morton, Doris. RALPH WALDO EMERSON AND THE DIAL: A STUDY IN LITERARY CRITICISM. Emporia State Research Studies, vol. 18, no. 2. Emporia: Kansas State Teachers College, 1969.

> "Emerson believed that, as editor, critic, and contributor, he could develop taste in his readers, provide new critical guidelines, and influence young writers to trust their insight and to avoid imitation."

Murphy, Michael E. "Meredith's 'Essay on Comedy': a Possible Source." NOTES AND QUERIES, 11 (1964), 228.

> A passage in Volume IV of THE DIAL possibly served as a source for Meredith's essay thirty-four years later.

Myerson, Joel. "An Annotated List of Contributions to the Boston DIAL." STUDIES IN BIBLIOGRAPHY, 26 (1973), 133-66.

Myerson uses new sources of information, such as attributions in contemporary letters and journals, in order to improve on previous lists of contributors to the four volumes of THE DIAL.

_____. "A History of the DIAL (1840-1844)." Dissertation, Northwestern University, 1971.

Perkins, Norman C. "The Original 'Dial.'" THE DIAL, 1 (1880), 9-11.

Perkins briefly recounts the founding and history of THE DIAL and discusses a number of the magazine's contributors.

Pollin, Burton R. "Emerson's Annotations in the British Museum Copy of the DIAL." STUDIES IN BIBLIOGRAPHY, 24 (1971), 187-95.

This copy of THE DIAL contains Emerson's own annotations as to the authorship of the magazine's anonymous contributions. Pollin lists Emerson's attributions and compares them to George W. Cooke's list of contributors as well as the annotations written into the Harvard University file of the magazine. Discrepancies seem to be minor.

Pyre, J.F.A. "The 'Dial' of 1840-45." THE DIAL, 26 (1899), 297-300.

This account of THE DIAL's career maintains that the journal "holds some such place in the history of American magazines as the young Marcellus and Sir Philip Sidney occupy in the history of men: fascinating the imagination by the appeal of brilliant promise, early death, and pathetic unfulfilments."

Rosenthal, Bernard, "The DIAL, Transcendentalism, and Margaret Fuller." ENGLISH LANGUAGE NOTES, 8 (1970), 28-36.

Rosenthal stresses Margaret Fuller's dominant control of THE DIAL during its first two years in order to clear up the misconception that the journal was guided throughout its life by Emerson or the Transcendental group in general.

Rusk, Ralph L. THE LIFE OF RALPH WALDO EMERSON. New York: Charles Scribner's Sons, 1949.

Chapter XVII, "The DIAL and the Essays," views Emerson's DIAL work in the context of the other activities in which he was engaged at the time.

Russell, Phillips. EMERSON: THE WISEST AMERICAN. New York: Brentano's, 1929.

Chapter XIX (pp. 181-92) describes the founding of THE DIAL, Margaret Fuller's struggle as its editor, Emerson's reluctant assumption of the helm and his work there, and the journal's demise.

Stern, Madeleine B. THE LIFE OF MARGARET FULLER. New York: E.P. Dutton, 1942.

Chapter IX, "Shadows on the DIAL," covers Margaret Fuller's editorship of the journal, her relationship with Emerson and other contributors, and the critical reception of THE DIAL.

Wade, Mason. MARGARET FULLER: WHETSTONE OF GENIUS. New York: Viking Press, 1940.

Margaret Fuller's editorship of THE DIAL and the journal's contents and reputation are investigated in Chapter VI, "The 'Dial' and Emerson."

Warfel, Harry R. "Margaret Fuller and Ralph Waldo Emerson." PMLA, 50 (1935), 576-94.

Although Warfel states that "It is not our purpose here to appraise THE DIAL or Margaret's part in it except so far as it shows how she and Emerson were drawn together into more simple and direct relations," he does give a detailed account of their work on the journal.

Webster, Frank Martindale. "Transcendental Points of View: a Survey of the Criticism of Music, Art, and Letters in THE DIAL, 1840-44." WASHINGTON UNIVERSITY STUDIES, HUMANISTIC SERIES, 7 (1920), 187-203.

THE DIAL's criticism reflects the Transcendentalist outlook.

* * * * *

THE FARMER'S WEEKLY MUSEUM (1793-1810)

Aldrich, George. WALPOLE AS IT WAS AND AS IT IS, CONTAINING THE COMPLETE CIVIL HISTORY OF THE TOWN FROM 1749 TO 1879. Claremont, N.H.: Claremont Manufacturing Co., 1880.

Pp. 79-84 cover the founding of the FARMER'S MUSEUM and the characteristics of the literary club which wrote for it, including a curiously general tendency toward drunkeness among its members.

Peabody, Andrew P. "The FARMER'S WEEKLY MUSEUM." PROCEEDINGS OF THE AMERICAN ANTIQUARIAN SOCIETY, 6 (1889), 106-24.

David Carlisle started the MUSEUM in 1793, and Joseph Dennie served as editor from 1795 to 1799. This article discusses the magazine's contents and the activities of the men associated with it.

* * * * *

THE HARBINGER (1845-1849)

Frothingham, Octavius Brooks. GEORGE RIPLEY. 5th ed. Boston: Houghton, Mifflin, 1886.

Ripley's editorship of THE HARBINGER is briefly discussed, and on pp. 177-80 the journal's prospectus is reprinted in full.

Joyeaux, Georges J. "George Sand, Eugenie Sue and THE HARBINGER." FRENCH REVIEW, 27 (1953), 122-31.

>THE HARBINGER, edited by members of the Brook Farm community who advocated Fourierist social doctrines, published works by two French writers whose reformist views coincided with those of the magazine.

Poe, Edgar Allan. "Brook Farm." THE COMPLETE WORKS OF EDGAR ALLAN POE. Ed. James A. Harrison. New York: Thomas Y. Crowell, 1902. XIII, 27-32.

>In this piece from THE BROADWAY JOURNAL of December 13, 1845, Poe attacks the Brook Farm "Crazyites" who in THE HAR-BINGER criticized a published collection of his poems.

* * * * *

THE HARVARD ADVOCATE (1866-current)

THE HARVARD ADVOCATE ANTHOLOGY. Ed. Donald Hall. New York: Twayne, 1950.

>Hall's "Introduction" covers the magazine's founding in 1866 and the contents and policies since then. A short introduction to each writer included in the anthology reveals his association with the ADVOCATE.

* * * * *

THE HARVARD LAMPOON (1876-current)

Stimpson, Mary Stoyell. "The HARVARD LAMPOON: Its Founders and Famous Contributors." NEW ENGLAND MAGAZINE, 35 (1907), 579-90.

* * * * *

THE HARVARD LYCEUM (1810-1811)

Matthews, Albert. "A Projected Harvard Magazine, 1814." HARVARD GRAD-UATES' MAGAZINE, 37 (1929), 445-47.

>The LYCEUM, which endured from July 1810, to March 1811, was the first printed student periodical at Harvard. Matthews discovers that an unsuccessful attempt was made three years later to revive it.

* * * * *

LITTELL'S LIVING AGE (1844-1896), later THE LIVING AGE (1897-1941)

"Ninety Years On." THE LIVING AGE, 346 (1934), 198-224.

"An Historical Survey," which precedes some reprinted pieces from
past issues, surveys the periodical's history, including a discussion
of founder Eliakim Littell. The May 11, 1844, "Prospectus" is
also reprinted.

* * * * *

THE LOWELL OFFERING (1840-1845)

"THE LOWELL OFFERING." THE NORTH AMERICAN REVIEW, 52 (1841), 537-
40.

After perusing the first three issues of the periodical, the writer
praises them as evidence of the intelligence and industry of the
Lowell factory girls, and he includes an exemplary poem to support
his views.

* * * * *

THE MASSACHUSETTS MAGAZINE (1789-1796)

Brown, Herbert R. "Elements of Sensibility in THE MASSACHUSETTS MAGA-
ZINE." AMERICAN LITERATURE, 1 (1929), 286-96.

The MAGAZINE shows the influence of Richardson and Sterne.
With sentimental fiction and tales of seduction it became "a shrine
for literary ladies of Massachusetts."

_____. "Richardson and Sterne in the MASSACHUSETTS MAGAZINE." NEW
ENGLAND QUARTERLY, 5 (1932), 65-82.

Viewing the relatively long-lived periodical as reflective of the
taste of the American public, Brown notes the "strong bias for tales
of seduction, the vogue of sentiment and sensibility, the appeals
to 'female readers,' the didacticism" that, borrowed from English
authors, made the magazine a success.

Kaiser, Leo M. "Colonial American Renderings of Horace in THE MASSACHU-
SETTS MAGAZINE." CLASSICAL BULLETIN, 39 (1963), 81-83.

The magazine's references to and views of Horace are discussed.

* * * * *

THE MASSACHUSETTS QUARTERLY REVIEW (1847-1850)

Commager, Henry Steele. THEODORE PARKER. Boston: Little, Brown, 1936.

After discussing Parker's editorial activities for THE MASSACHUSETTS
QUARTERLY REVIEW on pp. 130-34, Commager concludes that "It
was, as Thomas Higginson remarked, not the DIAL with a beard,
but the beard without the DIAL. Perhaps its chief value was as
a vehicle for Parker's writing."

Frothingham, Octavius Brooks. THEODORE PARKER: A BIOGRAPHY. New York: G.P. Putnam's Sons, 1886.

> Pp. 395-98 cover Parker's stint as editor of the REVIEW. In addition, on p. 139 Frothingham notes a comparison Parker made between THE DIAL group and Orestes Brownson of THE BOSTON QUARTERLY REVIEW in which the former are seen as too vague and insubstantial.

*　*　*　*　*

THE MONITOR, OR, AMERICAN SATURDAY REVIEW (1862)

Cameron, Kenneth Walter. "Thoreau, Parker, and Emerson's 'Mousetrap' in THE MONITOR (1862)." EMERSON SOCIETY QUARTERLY, 7 (II Quarter 1957), 42-46.

> THE MONITOR, a short-lived and now obscure periodical published in Concord, contained articles, reprinted here, about Thoreau's death and about Theodore Parker. Cameron also reprints the front page of THE MONITOR's seventh and penultimate issue.

*　*　*　*　*

THE MONTHLY ANTHOLOGY AND BOSTON REVIEW (1803-1811)

THE FEDERALIST LITERARY MIND: SELECTIONS FROM THE MONTHLY ANTHOLOGY AND BOSTON REVIEW, 1803-1811, INCLUDING DOCUMENTS RELATING TO THE BOSTON ATHENAEUM. Ed. Lewis P. Simpson. Baton Rouge: Louisiana State University Press, 1962.

> The anthology is intended to present a portrait of the federalist literary mind, and the lengthy introduction examines the periodical's career, policies, and significance in American literary history, especially its role in the rise of Boston as a literary center.

Greene, Sue N. "The Contribution of THE MONTHLY ANTHOLOGY AND BOSTON REVIEW to the Development of the Golden Age of American Letters." Dissertation, Michigan State University, 1964.

Harrington, Richard P. "THE MONTHLY ANTHOLOGY AND BOSTON REVIEW, 1803-1811: Literary Excellence as Interpreted by 'A Society of Gentlemen.'" Dissertation, University of Texas, 1964.

JOURNAL OF THE PROCEEDINGS OF THE SOCIETY WHICH CONDUCTS THE MONTHLY ANTHOLOGY & BOSTON REVIEW, OCTOBER 3, 1805, TO JULY 2, 1811. Boston: The Boston Atheneum, 1910.

> In an introduction entitled "The Anthology Society and Its Minutes," M.A. DeWolfe Howe examines the publishing and editing history of THE MONTHLY ANTHOLOGY. He includes a favorable review of the periodical which was published in 1805 by Joseph Dennie in THE PORT FOLIO, as well as a final address by the editors which

appeared in the June 1811 ANTHOLOGY. Also included at the end of the volume are a collation of the magazine from its founding to its last issue and a list of contributors (pp. 305-28).

Simpson, Lewis P. "A Literary Adventure of the Early Republic: the Anthology Society and the MONTHLY ANTHOLOGY." NEW ENGLAND QUARTERLY, 27 (1954), 168-90.

Simpson examines the six-year history of the magazine.

* * * * *

THE NEW ENGLAND GALAXY (1817-1834)

Buckingham, Joseph T. "THE NEW ENGLAND GALAXY AND MASONIC MAGAZINE." PERSONAL MEMOIRS AND RECOLLECTIONS OF EDITORIAL LIFE. Boston: Ticknor, Reed, and Fields, 1852. I, 73-256.

The founder and editor of the GALAXY from 1817 to 1828 recounts in detail his experiences with the journal and its contributors. It survived under new ownership until 1834.

* * * * *

THE NEW ENGLAND MAGAZINE (1758)

Hall, Holman S. "The First NEW ENGLAND MAGAZINE." NEW ENGLAND MAGAZINE, 33 (1906), 520-25.

Hall reviews the first two issues of THE NEW ENGLAND MAGAZINE, now located in the Boston Public Library, in order to get a picture of colonial Boston literature.

* * * * *

THE NEW ENGLAND MAGAZINE (1831-1835)

Cooke, George Willis. "The First NEW ENGLAND MAGAZINE and Its Editor." THE NEW ENGLAND MAGAZINE, 16 (1897), 103-17.

A later periodical than the one discussed by Hall, this first attempt in New England of an illustrated magazine devoted to literature was begun in 1831 by Joseph T. Buckingham and his son Edwin, and ran until 1835, when it was merged with the New York AMERICAN MONTHLY MAGAZINE. Cooke reprints some of the contents, including excerpts from poems and essays by Oliver Wendell Holmes, and examines generally not only the journal's contents but also its policies and goals.

* * * * *

THE NORTH AMERICAN REVIEW (1815-1940)

Adams, Herbert B. THE LIFE AND WRITINGS OF JARED SPARKS. 2 vols.

Boston: Houghton, Mifflin, 1893.

Chapter VIII, "Editor of the 'North American Review' (1823–1830)," not only investigates Sparks' policies while editor of the journal, but gives information on earlier magazines in Massachusetts, as well as the Anthology Club and the Boston Athenaeum, all of which serves as useful background material relating to the REVIEW.

Benson, Adolph B. "The Essays of Fredrika Bremer in the NORTH AMERICAN REVIEW." PMLA, 41 (1926), 747–55.

Lowell and Longfellow apparently wrote three articles about the Swedish novelist that appeared in the REVIEW in 1843 and 1844.

Clark, Harry H. "Literary Criticism in the NORTH AMERICAN REVIEW, 1815–1835." TRANSACTIONS OF THE WISCONSIN ACADEMY OF SCIENCES, ARTS, AND LETTERS, 32 (1940), 299–350.

Clark briefly summarizes the contents of the REVIEW's articles.

"Contributions to the 'North American Review' from Its Commencement to the Present Time." HISTORICAL MAGAZINE, 3 (1859), 343–45.

The list of contributors is preceded by a survey of the publishing history of THE MONTHLY ANTHOLOGY and the REVIEW.

Cushing, William. INDEX TO THE NORTH AMERICAN REVIEW. VOLUMES I–CXXV. 1815–1877. Cambridge, Mass.: John Wilson and Son, 1878.

Cushing includes one index of subjects and one of writers.

DeMille, George E. "The Birth of the Brahmins." SEWANEE REVIEW, 37 (1929), 172–88.

THE NORTH AMERICAN REVIEW is surveyed from its inception to about 1850. DeMille feels that it pioneered the way for other periodicals such as THE SOUTHERN LITERARY MESSENGER and THE NEW YORK MIRROR.

_____. "THE NORTH AMERICAN REVIEW." LITERARY CRITICISM IN AMERICA: A PRELIMINARY SURVEY. 1931; rpt. New York: Russell & Russell, 1967. Pp. 17–48.

In this first chapter of his study DeMille traces the critical ideas which characterized the REVIEW to 1850. The ideas of REVIEW writers, including Francis Bowen and Edwin Percy Whipple, are considered important in the development of American literary criticism.

Dennis, G. Rodney. "Attributions of Critical Notices in the 'North American Review.'" PAPERS OF THE BIBLIOGRAPHICAL SOCIETY OF AMERICA, 58 (1964), 292–93.

This list supplements Cushing's INDEX by covering the years 1836

to 1842, the period for which Cushing was unable to obtain authorship information.

Drewry, John E. "NORTH AMERICAN REVIEW--America's Oldest Magazine."
CONTEMPORARY AMERICAN MAGAZINES: A SELECTED BIBLIOGRAPHY AND
REPRINTS OF ARTICLES DEALING WITH VARIOUS PERIODICALS. 3rd ed.
Athens: University of Georgia Press, 1938. Pp. 49-52.

This is a loosely-organized discussion of the journal's career, relying
heavily on Mott's studies and W.F. Johnson's biography of George
Harvey.

Farrior, John E. "A Study of the NORTH AMERICAN REVIEW: The First
Twenty Years." Dissertation, University of North Carolina, 1954.

Firda, Richard Arthur. "German Philosophy of History and Literature in the
NORTH AMERICAN REVIEW: 1815-1860." JOURNAL OF THE HISTORY OF
IDEAS, 32 (1971), 133-42.

Firda believes that American critical thought was influenced by the
REVIEW's attitudes toward German romantic ideas.

_____. "The NORTH AMERICAN REVIEW, 1815-1860: A Study in the Re-
ception of German-American Cultural Influences." Dissertation, Harvard University, 1967.

"From Madison to Wilson." THE NORTH AMERICAN REVIEW, 201 (1915), 1-
14.

The political milieu in 1815, the year of the REVIEW's founding,
is contrasted with that of 1915.

Frothingham, Paul Revere. EDWARD EVERETT: ORATOR AND STATESMAN.
Boston: Houghton, Mifflin, 1925.

Everett assumed editorship of the REVIEW in 1820, and pp. 67-69
briefly discuss his tenure.

Gatell, Frank Otto. JOHN GORHAM PALFREY AND THE NEW ENGLAND
CONSCIENCE. Cambridge, Mass.: Harvard University Press, 1963.

Chapter VI, "The NORTH AMERICAN," covers Palfrey's ownership
of the REVIEW from 1835 to 1842, the year he sold it to Francis
Bowen. The journal almost went bankrupt, and Gatell describes
this period of Palfrey's life as one of frustration and failure.

Hardy, Thomas. "A Hundred Years Since." THE NORTH AMERICAN REVIEW,
201 (1915), 173-74.

Hardy commemorates the journal's centenary with a poem.

Howells, William Dean. "Part of Which I Was." THE NORTH AMERICAN
REVIEW, 201 (1915), 135-41.

Howells writes of his personal involvement with the journal and gives his thoughts about its changes, among the most important of which were its move under Allen Thorndike Rice to New York and its change from a quarterly to a bi-monthly, and then to a monthly.

Kleinfield, H.L. "Infidel on Parnassus: Lord Byron and the NORTH AMERI-CAN REVIEW." NEW ENGLAND QUARTERLY, 33 (1960), 164-85.

Although Byron was popular in America during the first half of the nineteenth century, the REVIEW's critics saw him as a threat to their conservative aesthetic and attacked his work and his imitators.

Lodge, Henry Cabot. "This 'Review': A Reminiscence." THE NORTH AMERI-CAN REVIEW, 201 (1915), 749-56.

The writer considers his own relationship to the journal, which he had edited from 1873 to 1876, and various changes the REVIEW has gone through in its long career.

McDowell, Tremaine. "Bryant and THE NORTH AMERICAN REVIEW." AMERI-CAN LITERATURE, 1 (1929), 14-26.

During the crucial period from 1816 to 1821, when many of Bryant's friends were advising him to pursue a law career, the editors of the REVIEW encouraged him through the publication of his work and personal contact to pursue his interest in literature.

Miller, F. DeWolfe. "Identification of Contributors to the NORTH AMERICAN REVIEW under Lowell." STUDIES IN BIBLIOGRAPHY, 6 (1953-54), 219-29.

This is "a complementary index to the NORTH AMERICAN REVIEW, 1864-1872, which every researcher working with the REVIEW for that period should consult."

Mott, Frank Luther. "One Hundred and Twenty Years." THE NORTH AMERI-CAN REVIEW, 240 (1935), 144-74.

Unlike many articles commemorating journalistic anniversaries, this one presents a useful detailed survey of the periodical's 120-year history, including policy changes under various editors.

"The NORTH AMERICAN REVIEW." THE NORTH AMERICAN REVIEW, 201 (1915), 142-60, 303-18, 469-80, 629-40, 789-800.

A profile of the REVIEW is created through this collection of ex-cerpts from its past issues. Also included are portraits or photos of the REVIEW's editors along with brief summaries of their careers.

Paine, Gregory. "Cooper and THE NORTH AMERICAN REVIEW." STUDIES IN PHILOLOGY, 27 (1931), 799-809.

With its pro-American literary stance, the REVIEW eagerly welcomed Cooper's early novels, but later, especially under the editorship of the narrow-minded Francis Bowen (1843-1852), the REVIEW attacked him. Paine feels that the journal declined in quality under Bowen and J.G. Palfrey (1835-1842).

Phelps, William Lyon. "'Thanatopsis' in the NORTH AMERICAN REVIEW."
THE NORTH AMERICAN REVIEW, 201 (1915), 224-27.

> Phelps argues that the poem as it appeared in the REVIEW was not
> a juvenile work, but that important passages from it were not in-
> cluded. He also quotes from and praises "The Embargo," an early
> satirical poem by Bryant published in the periodical.

"The Semi-Centenary of the NORTH AMERICAN REVIEW." THE NORTH
AMERICAN REVIEW, 100 (1865), 315-30.

> This fiftieth-anniversary piece reviews the periodical's history through
> accounts by previous editors. The constant tone of praise, especial-
> ly in the account of Bowen's editorship, provides an interesting con-
> trast to Paine's views in his article about Cooper and the REVIEW.

Shrell, Darwin. "Nationalism and Aesthetics in the NORTH AMERICAN RE-
VIEW: 1815-1850." STUDIES IN AMERICAN LITERATURE. Eds. Waldo
McNeir and Leo B. Levy. Baton Rouge: Louisiana State University Press, 1960.
Pp. 11-21.

> The contents of the REVIEW during this period reflect the dilemma
> faced by American critics of reconciling literary nationalism with
> a literary aesthetic derived from England and the rest of Europe.

Spiker, Claude C. "The NORTH AMERICAN REVIEW and French Morals."
WEST VIRGINIA BULLETIN OF PHILOLOGICAL STUDIES, 4, Ser. 44 (September 1943), 3-14.

> The REVIEW's attitude toward French literature and ideas during the
> period from 1815 to 1861 is discussed.

Streeter, Robert E. "Association Psychology and Literary Nationalism in the
NORTH AMERICAN REVIEW, 1815-1825." AMERICAN LITERATURE, 17 (1945),
243-54.

> During the nationalistic period following the War of 1812, the RE-
> VIEW writers embraced the principles of association psychology to
> support the view that literature based on American ideas and loca-
> tions is the best fare for American readers.

_____. "Critical Thought in the NORTH AMERICAN REVIEW, 1815-1865."
Dissertation, Northwestern University, 1943.

Ward, Julius H. "The NORTH AMERICAN REVIEW." THE· NORTH AMERICAN
REVIEW, 201 (1915), 123-34.

> Ward reviews the hundred-year history of the periodical, often giving
> details of the contents of certain issues. Unlike most commemora-
> tive essays, this one is realistic in its appraisals, especially of the
> editorships of Bowen and his successor Peabody, under whom the
> REVIEW did not fare well.

*   *   *   *   *   *

OLD AND NEW (1870-1875)

Hale, Edward E., Jr. THE LIFE AND LETTERS OF EDWARD EVERETT HALE. 2 vols. Boston: Little, Brown, 1917.

> In Chapter XXII, "'Old and New,' 1869-1870," Hale's founding and editing of the magazine are covered. He desired it to be "a BLACKWOOD or an ATLANTIC, whose pervading tone will be as pure religion as we know of, instead of toryism as in BLACKWOOD, or literature as in the ATLANTIC."

Holloway, Jean. EDWARD EVERETT HALE: A BIOGRAPHY. Austin: University of Texas Press, 1956.

> Chapter XI on OLD AND NEW examines Hale's Unpaid editorship of the periodical from 1870 to 1875.

* * * * *

THE PILOT (1890-1905)

Lane, Roger, "James Jeffrey Roche and the Boston PILOT." NEW ENGLAND QUARTERLY, 33 (1960), 341-63.

> From 1890 to 1905 the young author and poet edited THE PILOT, a Catholic literary and political weekly. Lane discusses Roche's policies and the journal's contents during this period.

* * * * *

THE PIONEER (1843)

Bradley, Sculley. "Introduction." THE PIONEER: A LITERARY MAGAZINE. 1843; rpt. New York: Scholars' Facsimiles & Reprints, 1947.

> The "Introduction" views THE PIONEER in the context of the general situation of literary journals during this period, and its founding is seen as an apprenticeship for Lowell's later editing of the ATLANTIC. According to Bradley, Lowell and co-editor Robert Carter created the journal "to promote American, rather than foreign authorship, to foster objective criticism and fearless opinion while avoiding the prevailing use of literary reviews for blackguarding one's enemies and settling personal scores."

* * * * *

THE POST BOY (1850-1851)

McLendon, Will L. "Misshelved Americana: THE POST BOY." PAPERS OF THE BIBLIOGRAPHICAL SOCIETY OF AMERICA, 61 (1967), 343-47.

> THE POST BOY has been mistakenly included in the UNION LIST OF SERIALS as a British periodical. Internal evidence shows that Cambridge, Massachusetts, not Cambridge, England, was the place

of publication.

_____. "Lowell, Emerson, and the PIONEER." AMERICAN LITERATURE, 19 (1947), 231-44.

Bradley explores the reasons for THE PIONEER's failure after three issues, and he reveals some episodes occuring while Lowell was ill and his associate Carter was in charge of the journal that caused Lowell considerable embarrassment with Emerson.

Mabbott, T.O. "A Review of Lowell's Magazine." NOTES AND QUERIES, 178 (1940), 457-58.

A favorable review of THE PIONEER is attributed to Poe. It had been published anonymously on the cover of the journal's second issue.

Mead, Edwin D. "Lowell's PIONEER." NEW ENGLAND MAGAZINE, 5 (1891), 235-48.

Mead discusses the journal's contents, and he includes numerous excerpts, a few of the illustrations, and a reprint of the title page from the first issue.

* * * * * *

RIVERSIDE MAGAZINE FOR YOUNG PEOPLE (1867-1870)

Ballou, Ellen B. "Horace Elisha Scudder and the RIVERSIDE MAGAZINE." HARVARD LIBRARY BULLETIN, 14 (1960), 426-52.

The literary contents of this children's magazine are discussed, as well as Scudder's goals as editor. The article begins with a general survey of children's magazines in the first half of the nineteenth century.

* * * * * *

THE YOUTH'S COMPANION (1827-1929)

Harris, Louise. "NONE BUT THE BEST" OR THE STORY OF THREE PIONEERS, THE YOUTH'S COMPANION, DANIEL SHARP FORD, C.A. STEPHENS. Providence: C.A. Stephens Collection, Brown University, 1966.

Ford became editor of the COMPANION in 1857, and Stephens joined the staff in 1870 as traveller and writer. The entire history of the periodical is given here, from its founding by N.P. Willis in 1827 to its death in 1934. Chapters cover "Circulation and Management," "Advertising and Premiums," and "The Staff and Contributors." Included among the last are William Dean Howells, Jules Verne, Rudyard Kipling, and Sarah Orne Jewett.

Katz, Joseph. "Stephen Crane to YOUTH'S COMPANION: A New Letter." STEPHEN CRANE NEWSLETTER, 2 (Winter 1967), 5.

Crane replies positively to a request for contributions by the periodical.

Chapter 4

LITERARY PERIODICALS

OF THE MID-ATLANTIC STATES

Chapter 4

LITERARY PERIODICALS
OF THE MID-ATLANTIC STATES

General Studies

Baker, Portia. "Walt Whitman's Relations With Some New York Magazines."
AMERICAN LITERATURE, 7 (1935), 274-301.

> The attitudes toward Whitman in the following periodicals are exam-
> ined: THE SATURDAY PRESS, HARPER'S MONTHLY, SCRIBNER'S
> MONTHLY, THE ROUND TABLE, THE NATION, THE INDEPEN-
> DENT, and THE CRITIC. THE SATURDAY PRESS and THE CRITIC
> consistently praised the poet, but THE NATION and THE INDEPEN-
> DENT remained hostile throughout his career.

Barnes, Homer F. CHARLES FENNO HOFFMAN. New York: Columbia University Press, 1930.

> Hoffman either edited or contributed to a number of journals during
> the 1830's and 1840's, including THE NEW YORK AMERICAN,
> THE NEW YORKER, and THE LITERARY WORLD.

Beers, Henry A. NATHANIEL PARKER WILLIS. 1885; rpt. New York: AMS
Press, 1969.

> The most important of Willis' ventures into literary journalism were
> the CORSAIR and the NEW MIRROR, published in the late 1830's
> and early 1840's, and the more successful HOME JOURNAL, begun
> in 1845 by Willis and George Pope Morris. Chapters VI and VII
> cover these activities in detail.

Clark, David Lee. CHARLES BROCKDEN BROWN: PIONEER VOICE OF
AMERICA. Durham, N.C.: Duke University Press, 1952.

> Brown's editorship from 1799 to 1800 of THE MONTHLY MAGA-
> ZINE AND AMERICAN REVIEW, the publication of the New York
> Friendly Club, is examined in Chapter V, "Brown's First Attempt
> at Journalism." Chapter VIII, "Brown again Turns to Journalism,"
> examines first the struggles of early literary periodicals in general,
> and then Brown's editorship of THE LITERARY MAGAZINE AND

AMERICAN REGISTER in Philadelphia from 1803 to 1808, including his goals and policies.

Dowgray, John Gray Laird, Jr. "A History of Harper's Literary Magazines, 1850-1900." Dissertation, University of Wisconsin, 1956.

The role of these periodicals in the popularization of knowledge during the second half of the century is examined. HARPER'S MONTHLY receives the most attention.

Ellsworth, William Webster. "Some Literary Reminiscences." THE BOOKMAN, 49 (1919), 409-18, 669-77.

A former staff member of SCRIBNER'S MONTHLY (later the CENTURY), Ellsworth discusses various magazines and the literary figures he met during his career.

Godwin, Parke. A BIOGRAPHY OF WILLIAM CULLEN BRYANT. 2 vols. New York: D. Appleton, 1883.

Bryant contributed to a number of early literary periodicals and edited THE UNITED STATES REVIEW under various changes in title and mergers with other publications. Pp. 219-35 discuss this period in Bryant's career, including his struggle to keep the REVIEW going, and his own poetic contributions to it.

Hageman, John Frelinghuysen. "Chapter XVII: Newspapers and Magazines of Princeton." HISTORY OF PRINCETON AND ITS INSTITUTIONS. 2nd ed. Philadelphia: J.B. Lippincott, 1879. II, 54-65.

Among the periodicals briefly discussed are THE PRINCETON RELIGIOUS AND LITERARY GAZETTE, THE PRINCETON COURIER AND LITERARY REGISTER, and THE PRINCETONIAN, the last specifically described as "predominantly literary in its character."

Hastings, George Everett. THE LIFE AND WORKS OF FRANCIS HOPKINSON. Chicago: University of Chicago Press, 1926.

Hopkinson contributed to literary periodicals and edited THE COLUMBIAN MAGAZINE. Pp. 434-35 contain a chronological list of his contributions to THE COLUMBIAN and THE AMERICAN MUSEUM from January 1787, to September 1792. An appendix (pp. 475-80) lists literary works appearing in magazines from June 1758, to September 1, 1790, that "contain something to suggest his authorship."

"The History of a Publishing House, 1846-1894." SCRIBNER'S MAGAZINE, 16 (1894), 793-804.

Included in this history of the Scribner firm are brief discussions of its HOURS AT HOME, SCRIBNER'S MONTHLY, and SCRIBNER'S MAGAZINE.

Marble, Annie Russell. HERALDS OF AMERICAN LITERATURE: A GROUP OF PATRIOT WRITERS OF THE REVOLUTIONARY AND NATIONAL PERIODS. Chicago: University of Chicago Press, 1907.

> Chapters VI and VIII sketch the careers of Joseph Dennie and Charles Brockden Brown. The contents and policies of Dennie's PORT FOLIO are detailed, including his publication of work by John Quincy Adams and the English poet Thomas Moore. Brown's editorship of THE LITERARY MAGAZINE AND AMERICAN REGISTER is also discussed. A bibliography lists the literary magazines they were involved with as editors or contributors.

Miller, Perry. THE RAVEN AND THE WHALE: THE WAR OF WORDS AND WITS IN THE ERA OF POE AND MELVILLE. New York: Harcourt, Brace, 1956.

> Miller studies the literary battles centered in New York between the old guard conservatives, represented by magazines such as THE KNICKERBOCKER and the WHIG REVIEW, and the pro-American-literature group called Young America, led by Evert Duyckinck, whose LITERARY WORLD and DEMOCRATIC REVIEW voiced more liberal views. These battles had a dominant effect on the way Melville's work was reviewed and received in New York. Miller's study reveals much about the rivalries, often personal and vindictive, of the period's literary magazines.

"Northern Periodicals Versus the South." THE SOUTHERN QUARTERLY REVIEW, 10 (1854), 503-11.

> Specifically criticizing HARPER'S MONTHLY and PUTNAM'S MONTHLY, the writer complains that "Even the so-called literary journals, failing to draw the distinction between questions purely social and those involving politics in their bitterest phase, have at length entered the arena, and undertaken to animadvert upon the views and practice of an entire section of the American Union."

Oberholtzer, Ellis Paxson. THE LITERARY HISTORY OF PHILADELPHIA. Philadelphia: George W. Jacobs, 1906.

> One chapter covers Joseph Dennie's PORT FOLIO and another GRAHAM'S.

Poe, Edgar Allan. "The Literati of New York City." THE COMPLETE WORKS OF EDGAR ALLAN POE. Ed. James A. Harrison. New York: Thomas Y. Crowell, 1902. XV, 1-137.

> First published in 1846 as a series in GODEY'S LADY'S BOOK, these sketches reveal Poe's attitude toward, among other figures, N.P. Willis and two editors of THE KNICKERBOCKER, Charles Fenno Hoffman and Lewis Gaylord Clark. Poe also comments on other literary journals of New York City.

Pritchard, John Paul. LITERARY WISE MEN OF GOTHAM: CRITICISM IN NEW YORK, 1815-1860. Baton Rouge: Louisiana State University Press, 1963.

> In this examination of New York critical ideas, Pritchard reveals in detail the views expressed in various of the city's literary periodicals. On pp. 144-48 he specifically deals with the weekly, monthly, and quarterly magazines as the media in which this criticism appeared, and on pp. 161-65 he examines the "personality" projected by journals such as THE KNICKERBOCKER, PUTNAM'S, and the DEMOCRATIC REVIEW.

Sartain, John. THE REMINISCENCES OF A VERY OLD MAN, 1808-1897. New York: D. Appleton, 1899.

> As a former illustrator for GRAHAM'S, Sartain in chapters XIII and XIV gives his views of that periodical. He also recounts here the founding of his SARTAIN'S UNION MAGAZINE.

Scharf, J. Thomas, and Thompson Westcott. "Chapter XLVIII: The Press of Philadelphia." HISTORY OF PHILADELPHIA, 1609-1884. Philadelphia: L.H. Everts, 1884. Pp. 1958-2062.

> Newspapers and journals are discussed individually.

Seilhamer, George O. "Weekly Newspapers and Magazines." MEMORIAL HISTORY OF THE CITY OF PHILADELPHIA. Ed. John Russell Young. New York: New York History Co., 1898. II, 268-84.

> Among the literary periodicals surveyed are THE PORT FOLIO, GRAHAM'S, and those edited by Charles Brockden Brown. Seilheimer also examines the growing popularity of illustrated periodicals and ladies' magazines in the mid-nineteenth century.

Smyth, Albert H. THE PHILADELPHIA MAGAZINES AND THEIR CONTRIBUTORS: 1741-1850. Philadelphia: Robert M. Lindsay, 1892.

> Smyth thoroughly examines major and minor literary periodicals, from THE COLUMBIAN and THE AMERICAN MUSEUM to GRAHAM'S and SARTAIN'S UNION MAGAZINE. Neither footnotes nor bibliography is provided.

Stafford, John. THE LITERARY CRITICISM OF 'YOUNG AMERICA': A STUDY IN THE RELATIONSHIP OF POLITICS AND LITERATURE, 1837-1850. Berkeley: University of California Press, 1952.

> In his study of the literary theories of Young America, Stafford examines the group's periodicals, primarily the DEMOCRATIC REVIEW, as well as the chief publications of their opponents, the WHIG REVIEW and THE NEW YORK REVIEW. Chapter I, "Politics, Magazines, and Publishing," discusses these periodicals in light of the publishing conditions of the time.

Stearns, Bertha Monica. "Early Philadelphia Magazines for Ladies." PENN-
SYLVANIA MAGAZINE OF HISTORY AND BIOGRAPHY, 64 (1940), 479-91.

> During the years from 1792 to 1830 a number of magazines for
> ladies were published in Philadelphia that prepared an audience
> for later and more successful periodicals, especially GODEY'S
> LADY'S BOOK.

_____. "Philadelphia Magazines for Ladies: 1830-1860." PENNSYLVANIA
MAGAZINE OF HISTORY AND BIOGRAPHY, 69 (1945), 207-19.

> A number of minor periodicals are surveyed, all of which relied on
> the "time-honored formula of 'amusement and instruction.'"

_____. "A Speculation Concerning Charles Brockden Brown." PENNSYLVA-
NIA MAGAZINE OF HISTORY AND BIOGRAPHY, 59 (1935), 99-105.

> Stearns argues from internal evidence that Brown had a hand in
> the production. of two ladies' magazines published in 1792, 1793,
> and 1796, THE LADY'S MAGAZINE AND REPOSITORY OF EN-
> TERTAINING KNOWLEDGE and THE LADY AND GENTLEMAN'S
> POCKET MAGAZINE OF LITERATURE AND POLITE AMUSEMENT.

Stoddard, Richard Henry. RECOLLECTIONS PERSONAL AND LITERARY. Ed.
Ripley Hitchcock. New York: A.S. Barnes, 1903.

> Editor Lewis Gaylord Clark and his periodical are discussed in
> Chapter IV, "The New World and the KNICKERBOCKER MAGA-
> ZINE," and THE HOME JOURNAL is viewed in Chapter VI, "In-
> fluence of N.P. Willis." In addition, Stoddard's at times discon-
> certing experiences with Poe when he was editing THE BROADWAY
> JOURNAL are related in Chapter XI, "Meetings With Poe."

Stone, William Leete. "Newspapers and Magazines." MEMORIAL HISTORY
OF THE CITY OF NEW YORK, FROM ITS FIRST SETTLEMENT TO THE YEAR
1892. Ed. James Grant Wilson. New York: New York History Co., 1893.
IV, 133-64.

> Stone surveys the city's major periodicals, many of them literary.

Woodall, Guy R. "Robert Walsh's War with the New York Literati: 1827-
1836." TENNESSEE STUDIES IN LITERATURE, 15 (1970), 25-47.

> While editor of the Philadelphia NATIONAL GAZETTE AND LIT-
> ERARY REGISTER and THE AMERICAN QUARTERLY REVIEW from
> 1827 to 1836, Walsh attacked and was attacked in turn by the
> New York literary circle which included N.P. Willis of THE NEW-
> YORK MIRROR and Lewis Gaylord Clark of the KNICKERBOCKER.

Studies of Individual Periodicals

THE AMERICAN MUSEUM (1787-1792)

Sylvester, Howard Eugene. "THE AMERICAN MUSEUM, a Study of Prevailing Ideas in Late Eighteenth-Century America." Dissertation, University of Washington, 1954.

> The MUSEUM, edited by Mathew Carey and published in Philadelphia from 1787 to 1792, is viewed as a reflection of American social and cultural ideas.

*　*　*　*　*

THE AMERICAN QUARTERLY REVIEW (1827-1837)

Aderman, Ralph M. "Contributors to the AMERICAN QUARTERLY REVIEW, 1827-1833." STUDIES IN BIBLIOGRAPHY, 14 (1961), 163-76.

> Aderman uses the publisher's account book for information about payments by and contributors to the REVIEW during the first six years of its career. In footnotes he provides short biographical sketches of each writer.

THE COST BOOK OF CAREY & LEA, 1825-1838. Ed. David Kaser. Philadelphia: University of Pennsylvania Press, 1963.

> Pp. 285-97 list contributors to the REVIEW and payments made to them.

Woodall, Guy R. "More on the Contributors to THE AMERICAN QUARTERLY REVIEW (1827-1837)." STUDIES IN BIBLIOGRAPHY, 23 (1970), 199-207.

> Woodall lists authors of the periodical's anonymous articles.

*　*　*　*　*

THE AMERICAN REVIEW: A WHIG JOURNAL OF POLITICS, LITERATURE, ART AND SCIENCE (1845-1852)

Mulqueen, James E. "Conservatism and Criticism: The Literary Standards of American Whigs, 1845-1852." AMERICAN LITERATURE, 41 (1969), 355-72.

> The critical principles expressed in this journal, commonly called the WHIG REVIEW, are directly related to Whig political conservatism.

*　*　*　*　*

THE ANALECTIC MAGAZINE (1813-1821)

Williams, Stanley T. THE LIFE OF WASHINGTON IRVING. 2 vols. 1935; rpt. New York: Octagon Books, 1971.

Chapter VI, "Editor and Officer," recounts Irving's difficulties as editor of the ANALECTIC from 1811 to 1813, and also describes the magazine's policies, contents, and early publishing history.

* * * * *

ARCTURUS (1840-1842)

Mabbott, Thomas Ollive. "ARCTURUS and Keats: An Early American Publication of Keats's 'La Belle Dame sans Merci.'" AMERICAN LITERATURE, 2 (1931), 430-32.

> Keats' poem appeared in the short-lived but highly-reputable New York ARCTURUS in January 1842, thus finding in America a "fit audience...though few."

* * * * *

THE BROADWAY JOURNAL (1845-1846)

Ehrlich, Heyward. "The BROADWAY JOURNAL: Briggs's Dilemma and Poe's Strategy." BULLETIN OF THE NEW YORK PUBLIC LIBRARY, 73 (1969), 74-93.

> This article examines the feud between editor Poe and Charles F. Briggs, the JOURNAL's original owner.

Rede, Kenneth. "Poe Notes: From an Investigator's Notebook." AMERICAN LITERATURE, 5 (1933), 49-54.

> Among these items is a complete copy of Poe's 1845 agreement with Thomas H. Lane in which Poe transferred half interest in THE BROADWAY JOURNAL.

Weidman, Bette S. "THE BROADWAY JOURNAL (2): A Casualty of Abolition Politics." BULLETIN OF THE NEW YORK PUBLIC LIBRARY, 73 (1969), 94-113.

> The JOURNAL's failure was not due entirely to Poe's policies, or to financial problems, as many critics have maintained. In fact, the magazine's anti-slavery but anti-abolitionist stand, established before Poe's editorship, resulted in fatal attacks by various political factions.

* * * * *

BURTON'S GENTLEMAN'S MAGAZINE (1837-1840)

C.E.W. "Poeana." AMERICAN BOOK COLLECTOR, 2 (1932), 348-52.

> The contents of BURTON'S are discussed as well as Poe's editorship of the magazine.

* * * * *

THE COLUMBIAN LADY'S AND GENTLEMAN'S MAGAZINE (1844-1849)

Williams, Mentor L. "Paulding's Contributions to the COLUMBIAN MAGA-
ZINE." AMERICAN LITERATURE, 21 (1949), 222-27.

> Paulding contributed "sentimental junk" to the magazine during its
> existence from 1844 to 1849.

_____. "Portrait of a Popular Journal: THE COLUMBIAN LADY'S AND
GENTLEMAN'S MAGAZINE." BULLETIN OF THE NEW YORK PUBLIC LIBRARY,
56 (1952), 3-17.

> This study examines the journal's contents and publishing history.

* * * * *

THE COLUMBIAN MAGAZINE (1786-1792)

Free, William J. "American Fiction in the COLUMBIAN MAGAZINE, 1786-
1792: An Annotated Checklist." BULLETIN OF BIBLIOGRAPHY, 25 (1968),
150-51.

> This article includes a list of twenty-eight "native" short stories,
> "indicates their location, and, where known, author and briefly
> describes their contents in the hope that future historians of Ameri-
> can culture will be able to make fuller use of this untapped re-
> source."

_____. THE COLUMBIAN MAGAZINE AND AMERICAN LITERARY NATION-
ALISM. The Hague: Mouton, 1968.

> The contents of THE COLUMBIAN MAGAZINE reveal the beginning
> of the long struggle to achieve a distinctly American literature.
> This is a thorough study of the magazine and its influence on the
> literary scene.

_____. "The COLUMBIAN MAGAZINE and Its Contribution to American
Literary Nationalism." Dissertation, University of North Carolina, 1962.

Mayo, Lawrence S. "Belknap and John Quincy Adams." PROCEEDINGS OF
THE MASSACHUSETTS HISTORICAL SOCIETY, 59 (1926), 203-10.

> This article contains a letter from Jeremy Belknap requesting a
> contribution from Adams for THE COLUMBIAN.

* * * * *

THE CONTINENT (1882-1884), entitled OUR CONTINENT during the first year

Dibble, Roy F. ALBION W. TOURGEE. New York: Lemke & Buechner,
1921.

> In 1882 Tourgee undertook, in his own words, "the first serious at-
> tempt ever made to put into a weekly the attractions and excel-

lences of our great monthlies." Chapter IV, "Our Continent," discusses the two-year life of the journal.

Gross, Theodore L. ALBION W. TOURGEE. New York: Twayne, 1963.

Pp. 106-8 examine Tourgee's policies as editor. OUR CONTIN-ENT is seen as "a turning point in his career: it clearly indicates the increasingly sentimental and commercial attitude Tourgee was to assume in his later fiction."

Olsen, Otto H. CARPETBAGGER'S CRUSADE: THE LIFE OF ALBION WINE-GAR TOURGEE. Baltimore: Johns Hopkins Press, 1965.

Chapter XX, "The CONTINENT Disaster," covers Tourgee's found-ing of his weekly journal, his goals, and the reasons for the fail-ure of the project. This investigation is more thorough than Dib-ble's or Gross'. In addition, pp. 332-34 discuss his short-lived Buffalo weekly, the BASIS.

*   *   *   *   *

COSMOPOLITAN MAGAZINE (1886-1925)

Brocki, Sister Mary Damascene, CSSF. "A Study of COSMOPOLITAN MAGA-ZINE, 1890-1900: Its Relation to the Literature of the Decade." Dissertation, University of Notre Dame, 1959.

Through its criticism and fiction, COSMOPOLITAN had a signifi-cant influence on the literary trends of the 1890's.

Rein, D.M. "Howells and the COSMOPOLITAN." AMERICAN LITERATURE, 21 (1949), 49-55.

Howells edited the May and June 1892 issues of the periodical, and these contain twice the amount of literary material found in issues before or after.

*   *   *   *   *

THE GALAXY (1866-1878)

Mott, Frank Luther. "The GALAXY: An Important American Magazine." SEWANEE REVIEW, 36 (1928), 86-103.

Counting Mark Twain among its editors and Henry James among its contributors during its existence from 1866 to 1878, THE GALAXY is important because "First, it was fresher and more lively and readable than most of the other periodicals of its day; second, it presents to the intelligent reader a better history of its times than any other monthly of the years from 1865 to 1880, because of its superior variety and directness; and third, it published a consider-able amount of important literature."

Pearson, Justus Richard. "THE GALAXY, 1866-1878." Dissertation, Columbia

University, 1955.

>Pearson studies the publication history of the magazine as well as its reflection of the culture of the period.

_____. "Story of a Magazine: New York's GALAXY 1866-1878. A Study Based on the Unpublished Correspondence of Its Editors." BULLETIN OF THE NEW YORK PUBLIC LIBRARY, 61 (1957), 217-37, 281-302.

>The journal's history is surveyed.

* * * * * *

GODEY'S LADY'S BOOK (1830-1898)

Finley, Ruth E. THE LADY OF GODEY'S: SARAH JOSEPHA HALE. Philadelphia: J.B. Lippincott, 1931.

>This study focuses on Mrs. Hale, whose editorial career started with her LADIES' MAGAZINE in 1828 and ended with her last issue of GODEY'S in 1877. However, Finley also presents much information about the magazine itself and Godey, the owner.

Martin, Lawrence. "The Genesis of Godey's 'Lady's Book.'" NEW ENGLAND QUARTERLY, 1 (1928), 41-70.

>When Mrs. Hale combined her LADIES' MAGAZINE with Godey's enterprise, she brought a crusading spirit that gave life to a mediocre magazine.

Mott, Frank Luther. "The Banquet of the Boudoir." SATURDAY REVIEW OF LITERATURE, 6 (1929), 441.

>The contributors and contents of GODEY'S are discussed here, with emphasis on the magazine's sentimentality. This discussion is included in Mott's A HISTORY OF AMERICAN MAGAZINES.

Satterwhite, Joseph N. "GODEY'S LADY'S BOOK and Fiction: 1830-1850." Dissertation, Vanderbilt University, 1954.

>The contents of GODEY'S indicate the popular taste of the day and reveal the literary milieu in which Hawthorne's and Melville's work should be viewed.

_____. "The Tremulous Formula: Form and Technique in GODEY'S Fiction." AMERICAN QUARTERLY, 8 (1956), 99-113.

>Satterwhite criticizes the sentimental fiction in GODEY'S, "the first successful American magazine to depend primarily on fiction for its content," and he finds it ironic that Poe published literary criticism in the periodical.

Sherrer, Grace Bussing. "French Culture as Presented to Middle-Class America by GODEY'S LADY'S BOOK, 1830-1840." AMERICAN LITERATURE, 3 (1931), 277-86.

GODEY'S published literature relating to French culture, although carefully stripped of any indelicacy, and as a result helped to usher in a period of interest in things French which lasted for another twenty years.

Tarbell, Ida M. "The American Woman: Those Who Did Not Fight." AMERICAN, 69 (1910), 656-69.

Pp. 666-68 cover the editorial career of Sarah Josepha Hale.

Warner, Richard Fay. "Godey's Lady's Book." AMERICAN MERCURY, 2 (1924), 399-405.

This is a sketch of GODEY'S history from 1830 to 1877, with wry commentary at times.

Woodward, Helen. THE LADY PERSUADERS. New York: Ivan Obolensky, 1960.

Sarah Josepha Hale and GODEY'S are discussed in Chapter III, "Fighting with Feather-Duster Prose."

Wright, Richardson. "The Madonna in Bustles." FORGOTTEN LADIES: NINE PORTRAITS FROM THE AMERICAN FAMILY ALBUM. Philadelphia: J.B. Lippincott, 1928. Pp. 187-217.

Wright discusses Mrs. Hale's work as editor of THE LADIES' MAGAZINE and then GODEY'S, concentrating on her efforts in the feminist movement.

*   *   *   *   *

GRAHAM'S MAGAZINE (1841-1858)

Mott, Frank Luther. "A Brief History of GRAHAM'S MAGAZINE." STUDIES IN PHILOLOGY, 25 (1928), 362-75.

The journal's history is examined in detail from its founding as the combined ATKINSON'S CASKET and GENTLEMAN'S MAGAZINE in 1839 to its decline in the 1850's. Poe's work as literary editor is also discussed.

Robbins, J. Albert, Jr. "George R. Graham, Philadelphia Publisher." PENNSYLVANIA MAGAZINE OF HISTORY AND BIOGRAPHY, 75 (1951), 279-94.

Robbins supplies the publishing facts and editorial policies of GRAHAM'S.

_____. "The History of GRAHAM'S MAGAZINE: A Study in Periodical Publication." Dissertation, University of Pennsylvania, 1947.

Thompson, Lawrance R. "Longfellow Sells THE SPANISH STUDENT." AMERICAN LITERATURE, 6 (1934), 141-50.

After rejections by several publishers, Longfellow published THE

SPANISH STUDENT in GRAHAM'S in 1842, and consequently became a regular contributor to the journal.

* * * * *

HARPER'S MONTHLY MAGAZINE (1850-current)

Alden, Henry Mills. "Editor's Study." HARPER'S MONTHLY, 119 (1909), 961-64.

> In surveying the history of HARPER'S, Alden defends its early practice of reprinting English literature.

_____. "Editor's Study." HARPER'S MONTHLY, 132 (1915), 152-54.

The editor protests the chapter of Tassin's study of American magazines which labels HARPER'S "The Converted Corsair," referring to the periodical's earlier practice of reprinting British literature without permission of the authors.

_____. "Fifty Years of HARPER'S MAGAZINE." HARPER'S MONTHLY, 100 (1900), 947-62.

> This is a reminiscence about editors, contributors, and events involving the periodical, with information on various departments that have been added and dropped.

Allen, Frederick Lewis. "One Hundred Years of HARPER'S." HARPER'S MONTHLY, 201 (October 1950), 23-36.

> Allen traces the publication's history, emphasizing the quality of its contents and the ability of its owners and editors to overcome problems such as a fire in 1853 and the rise of the cheap magazines in the 1890's. This piece was revised and published as "HARPER'S MAGAZINE" 1850-1950: A CENTENARY ADDRESS. New York: Newcomen Society in North America, 1950.

Canby, Henry Seidel. HARPER'S MAGAZINE--A NATIONAL INSTITUTION. New York: Harper and Brothers, 1925.

Davis, Elmer. "Constant Reader." HARPER'S MONTHLY, 201 (October 1950), 161-72.

> Davis reminisces about his childhood reading of HARPER'S.

Dowgray, John G.L., Jr. "Literature and History: HARPER'S MONTHLY--The Magazine and the Popularization of Knowledge." LITERATURE AND HISTORY. Ed. I.E. Cadenhead, Jr. Tulsa, Okla.: University of Tulsa, 1970. Pp. 88-101.

> During the time when periodicals were the principal means of cultural communication, HARPER'S worked to improve the level of taste and knowledge of a large middle-class reading public.

Drewry, John E. "HARPER'S Magazine--Where Ideas Are Hatched." CON-
TEMPORARY AMERICAN MAGAZINES: A SELECTED BIBLIOGRAPHY AND RE-
PRINTS OF ARTICLES DEALING WITH VARIOUS PERIODICALS. 3rd ed. Ath-
ens: University of Georgia Press, 1938. Pp. 27-30.

> This is a general discussion of the journal's founding, its history,
> and its contemporary characteristics.

Exman, Eugene. THE BROTHERS HARPER: A UNIQUE PUBLISHING PARTNER-
SHIP AND ITS IMPACT UPON THE CULTURAL LIFE OF AMERICA FROM 1817
TO 1853. New York: Harper & Row, 1965.

> Chapter XVII, "The New Monthly Magazine, 1850-1853," covers
> the periodical's history from its founding to the fire which destroyed
> the company's offices.

_____. THE HOUSE OF HARPER: ONE HUNDRED AND FIFTY YEARS OF
PUBLISHING. New York: Harper & Row, 1967.

> Chapter VII, "Harper's New Monthly Magazine (1850-1900)," and
> Chapter XXI, "HARPER'S MAGAZINE (1900-1967)," trace the jour-
> nal's history from its founding, including its successful struggle for
> survival against the cheap magazines around 1900.

GENTLEMEN, SCHOLARS AND SCOUNDRELS: A TREASURY OF THE BEST OF
HARPER'S MAGAZINE FROM 1850 TO THE PRESENT. Ed. Horace Knowles.
New York: Harper and Brothers, 1959. Latest of numerous editions from 1915.

> John Fischer's "Introduction" reviews the journal's founding, dis-
> cusses its goals, and notes some of its accomplishments. The vol-
> ume itself serves as a portrait of HARPER'S from its early years.

Harper, Henry J. THE HOUSE OF HARPER: A CENTURY OF PUBLISHING IN
FRANKLIN SQUARE. New York: Harper and Brothers, 1912.

> Chapter IX is devoted to a general discussion, almost an adoration,
> of HARPER'S. Its contents and contributors are mentioned at various
> times throughout the book.

Howells, William Dean. "Editor's Easy Chair." HARPER'S MONTHLY, 135
(1917), 138-41.

> On the occasion of the publishing house's hundredth anniversary
> and the magazine's sixty-seventh, Howells looks back with praise
> at the periodical's history.

_____. "In Memoriam." HARPER'S MONTHLY, 140 (1919), 133-36.

> Howells praises Alden and gives an inside, anecdotal view of Al-
> den's long career as editor of HARPER'S.

Kouwenhoven, John A. "America on the Move: How It Looked to the Authors
and illustrators of HARPER'S." HARPER'S MONTHLY, 201 (October 1950), 97-144.

> This is a collection, with commentary, of illustrations from through-

out the journal's history, especially the early years. It shows the quality and the importance of illustration in HARPER'S.

_____. "Personal & Otherwise." HARPER'S MONTHLY, 201 (October 1950), 8-20.

In this commemorative issue Kouwenhoven takes an overview of the magazine's history and sees three major phases--the period of visual description, roughly from 1850 to 1880; of interpretive sensibility from 1880 to 1920; and finally of insight and analysis.

Lutwack, Leonard. "William Dean Howells and the 'Editor's Study.'" AMERI-CAN LITERATURE, 24 (1952), 195-207.

Howells' contributions to the "Editor's Study" in HARPER'S beginning in 1886, and his later associations with the publication, offered him a greater opportunity to write quality literary criticism than had his earlier reviews as editor of the ATLANTIC.

West, Rebecca. "Reader, Transatlantic." HARPER'S MONTHLY, 201 (October 1950), 77-87.

An English reader and contributor discusses the periodical's relation to American and world culture. For instance she notes that the travel literature became Europe-oriented and the fiction more na-tionalistic.

* * * * *

HEARTH AND HOME (1868-1875)

Eggleston, George Cary. RECOLLECTIONS OF A VARIED LIFE. New York: Henry Holt, 1910.

As managing editor Eggleston, along with his brother Edward, guided the policies of HEARTH AND HOME from 1871 to 1874. Pp. 131-80 cover his association with this weekly journal, including his re-sulting friendships with Mary Mapes Dodge and Frank Stockton, both of whom later worked on the ST. NICHOLAS.

Randel, William Peirce. EDWARD EGGLESTON: AUTHOR OF THE HOOSIER SCHOOL-MASTER. New York: King's Crown Press, 1946.

Pp. 117-21 cover Eggleston's association with HEARTH AND HOME both as editor and contributor. Serialization of THE HOOSIER SCHOOL-MASTER in the magazine helped to establish his literary reputation.

* * * * *

THE KNICKERBOCKER MAGAZINE (1833-1863)

Clark, Lewis Gaylord. "Editorial Narrative of the KNICKERBOCKER MAGA-ZINE: Reminiscences of the Sanctum and of Our Correspondents." THE KNICK-

ERBOCKER, 53 (1859), 193-200, 308-12, 420-24, 640-47; 54 (1859), 94-103, 317-20, 424-31, 541-48; 55 (1860), 85-90, 215-21, 324-35, 430-38, 541-48, 643-52; 56 (1860), 86-99, 197-212, 418-25, 642-47; 57 (1861), 99-107, 224-29, 331-40, 442-46, 551-56; 58 (1861), 72-79.

> Clark, editor of THE KNICKERBOCKER, reminisces about the personalities and events of his long reign.

Spivey, Herman E. "THE KNICKERBOCKER MAGAZINE, 1833-1865: A Study of Its Contents, History, and Significance." Dissertation, University of North Carolina, 1935.

Thorpe, T.B. "Lewis Gaylord Clark." HARPER'S MONTHLY, 48 (1874), 587-92.

> Thorpe praises Clark's editorial work, sketches his life, and relates a number of anecdotes.

*   *   *   *   *

THE LARK (1895-1897)

Wells, Carolyn. "What a Lark!" COLOPHON, Part 8. October 1931.

> A former contributor tells of the little magazine's founders, Bruce Porter and Gelett Burgess, and prints a letter from Burgess explaining why he and Porter started the journal in 1895 as well as why he decided to leave it two years later.

*   *   *   *   *

LIFE (1883-1936)

DaPonte, Durant. "LIFE Reviews HUCKLEBERRY FINN." AMERICAN LITERATURE, 31 (1959), 78-81.

> A previously unknown review, here reprinted in full, misses the novel's significance completely.

Hagemann, E.R. "LIFE Buffets and (Comforts) Henry James, 1883-1916: An Introduction and An Annotated Checklist." PAPERS OF THE BIBLIOGRAPHICAL SOCIETY OF AMERICA, 62 (1968), 207-25.

> LIFE satirized and parodied, yet also praised, James during this period. Hagemann also sketches the magazine's history, concluding with a lengthy "Annotated Check List of Jamesiana in LIFE" (pp. 211-25).

Mott, Frank Luther. "Fifty Years of LIFE: The Story of a Satirical Weekly." JOURNALISM QUARTERLY, 25 (1948), 224-32.

> This survey of the magazine's history also appears in Volume IV of Mott's A HISTORY OF AMERICAN MAGAZINES.

Silver, Rollo G. "Concerning Walt Whitman." NOTES AND QUERIES, 167 (1934), 96.

> In 1856 two articles by Whitman appeared in LIFE.

* * * * *

M'LLE NEW YORK (1895-1896, 1898-1899)

Hanighen, Frank C. "Vance Thompson and M'LLE NEW YORK." THE BOOK-MAN, 75 (1932), 472-81.

> Influenced by THE CHAP-BOOK and the English YELLOW BOOK, Thompson founded his short-lived magazine in protest against the prevailing prudery in American literary periodicals. Some of the magazine's illustrations are included.

* * * * *

THE MONTHLY MAGAZINE, AND AMERICAN REVIEW (1799-1800), later THE AMERICAN REVIEW, AND LITERARY JOURNAL (1801-1802)

Clark, David Lee. "Brockden Brown's First Attempt at Journalism." UNIVERSITY OF TEXAS STUDIES IN ENGLISH, 7 (1927), 155-74.

> THE MONTHLY MAGAZINE, sponsored by the New York Friendly Club, was edited by Brown in 1799 and 1800.

Spiller, Robert E., ed. THE AMERICAN LITERARY REVOLUTION, 1783-1837. New York: New York University Press, 1967.

> Charles Brockden Brown's preface to THE AMERICAN REVIEW AND LITERARY JOURNAL FOR THE YEAR 1801 is reprinted on pp. 32-37.

Warfel, Harry R. CHARLES BROCKDEN BROWN: AMERICAN GOTHIC NOVELIST. Gainesville: University of Florida Press, 1949.

> Chapter XIV, "The MONTHLY MAGAZINE & AMERICAN REVIEW," relates how Brown optimistically helped found the MONTHLY in 1799, but was forced to admit failure in December 1800, because of lack of public support.

* * * * *

THE NEW JERSEY MAGAZINE (1786-1787)

Amacher, Richard E. "New Jersey's First Magazine." JOURNAL OF THE RUTGER'S UNIVERSITY LIBRARY, 12 (1948), 28-31.

> Amacher examines the only three issues printed of THE NEW JERSEY MAGAZINE (December 1786 to February 1787), and notes among other things the heavy imitation of English neoclassical literature.

* * * * *

THE NEW YORK LEDGER (1851-1887)

Admari, Ralph. "Bonner And 'The Ledger.'" AMERICAN BOOK COLLECTOR, 6 (1935), 176-93.

> Admari investigates the story paper phenomenon, the career of Robert Bonner, and the history, contents, and success of Bonner's weekly LEDGER, published from 1851 until his retirement in 1887.

*   *   *   *   *

NEW-YORK MAGAZINE (1790-1797)

Bowman, Mary Rives. "Dunlap and the 'Theatrical Register' of the NEW-YORK MAGAZINE." STUDIES IN PHILOLOGY, 24 (1927), 413-25.

> Evidence indicates that critic William Dunlap wrote "The Theatrical Register" for NEW-YORK MAGAZINE from November 1794 to April 1796.

*   *   *   *   *

THE NEW YORK MIRROR (1823-1847)

Johnson, Stanley. "How a New York Editor Was Accustomed to Give Out Advice." THE BOOKMAN, 26 (1907), 421-23.

> Editor N.P. Willis gave notice of manuscript rejections in the MIRROR itself, often with rudeness and ridicule.

*   *   *   *   *

THE NEW YORK WEEKLY REVIEW (1865-1873)

Carter, Paul J. "Mark Twain Material in the 'New York Weekly Review.'" PAPERS OF THE BIBLIOGRAPHICAL SOCIETY OF AMERICA, 52 (1958), 56-62.

> Twain published eight pieces in the REVIEW from 1865 to 1867. This fact "reveals Twain's active interest in Eastern outlets; second, it shows his early popularity with Eastern editors; and third, it signifies his acceptance by a relatively high-class paper."

*   *   *   *   *

THE NORTHERN MONTHLY AND NEW JERSEY MAGAZINE (1867-1868)

Eddy, Spencer L., Jr. "THE NORTHERN MONTHLY AND NEW JERSEY MAGAZINE: May 1867-June 1868." JOURNAL OF THE RUTGERS UNIVERSITY LIBRARY, 30 (1967), 40-52.

> Eddy sketches the history of this short-lived magazine.

*   *   *   *   *

NORTON'S LITERARY GAZETTE (1852-1855)

Krummel, Donald W. "The Library World of NORTON'S LITERARY GAZETTE."
BOOKS IN AMERICA'S PAST: ESSAYS HONORING RUDOLPH H. GJELSNESS.
Ed. David Kaser. Charlottesville: University of Virginia Press, 1966. Pp.
238-65.

> The contents of the GAZETTE were especially directed toward
> librarians, and Krummel examines the journal's views of American
> libraries and related matters.

*   *   *   *   *

THE PHILADELPHIA SATURDAY MUSEUM (1843)

Hutcherson, Dudley. "THE PHILADELPHIA SATURDAY MUSEUM Text of Poe's
Poems." AMERICAN LITERATURE, 5 (1933), 36-48.

> Twenty of Poe's poems were published for the first time in their
> final form in both the February 25, and March 4, 1843, issues of
> the MUSEUM. The event is important because this was "the only
> publication between 1831 and 1845 approximating an edition of
> Poe's poetry."

*   *   *   *   *

THE PORT FOLIO (1801-1827)

Bent, S. Arthur. "Damon and Pythias Among Our Early Journalists." NEW
ENGLAND MAGAZINE, 14 (1896), 666-75.

> This article traces the career of Joseph Dennie, including his ed-
> itorships of first the FARMER'S MUSEUM in Walpole, New Hamp-
> shire, and then of THE PORT FOLIO.

Kerber, Linda K., and Walter John Morris. "Politics and Literature: The Adams
Family and the PORT FOLIO." WILLIAM AND MARY QUARTERLY, 3rd Ser.,
23 (1966), 450-76.

> Without the encouragement of the Adams family THE PORT FOLIO
> probably would not have survived beyond its first three years. Pp.
> 467-76 list material contributed by members of the family.

Queenan, John T. "The PORT FOLIO: A Study of the History and Significance of an Early American Magazine." Dissertation, University of Pennsylvania, 1954.

> Queenan examines the contents and policies of THE PORT FOLIO
> throughout its career from 1801 to 1827 in order to determine the
> reasons for its success.

Randall, Randolph C. "Authors of the PORT FOLIO Revealed by the Hall
Files." AMERICAN LITERATURE, 11 (1940), 379-416.

The Hall brothers, editors of the periodical after Dennie, recorded in their files the authors of anonymous articles that appeared before and during their editorship. Among Randall's discoveries are some previously unknown pieces by John Quincy Adams.

_____. "Joseph Dennie's Literary Attitudes in the PORT FOLIO, 1801-1812." ESSAYS MOSTLY ON PERIODICAL PUBLISHING IN AMERICA. Durham, N.C.: Duke University Press, 1973. Pp. 57-91.

This article explains Dennie's conservative political views and then discusses his attitudes toward Rousseau, Wordsworth, Coleridge, Addison, Goldsmith, and Cowper.

Woodall, Guy R. "The Relationship of Robert Walsh, Jr., to the PORT FOLIO and the Dennie Circle: 1803-1812." PENNSYLVANIA MAGAZINE OF HISTORY AND BIOGRAPHY, 92 (1968), 195-219.

Walsh, later editor of the conservative AMERICAN QUARTERLY REVIEW, received valuable experience as a contributor to Dennie's journal. Woodall also studies Walsh's editorship of other periodicals including THE AMERICAN REVIEW OF HISTORY AND POLITICS, AND GENERAL REPOSITORY OF STATE PAPERS.

* * * * *

PUTNAM'S MONTHLY MAGAZINE (1853-1857, 1868-1870)

Harvey, Charles M. "A Memorable Half-Century: 1857-1907." PUTNAM'S, 7 (1910), 589-98.

Harvey considers the reaction of PUTNAM'S to the social and economic conditions of its time.

Kotzin, Miriam Naomi. PUTNAM'S MONTHLY and Its Place in American Literature." Dissertation, New York University, 1969.

Kotzin examines the literary contents of PUTNAM'S first series from 1853 to 1857, and places the journal in its literary and historical milieu.

M.S. "The Old PUTNAM'S." PUTNAM'S MONTHLY AND THE CRITIC, 1 (1906), 1-11.

In this reminiscence a former reader of PUTNAM'S discusses its varied contents and its contributors: "Was ever an American magazine launched under more brilliant literary auspices, or with a list of contributors so readily recognizable half a century later?"

Maddox, Notley S. "Literary Nationalism in PUTNAM'S MAGAZINE, 1853-1857." AMERICAN LITERATURE, 14 (1942), 117-25.

Throughout its career from 1853 to 1857, and again from 1868 to 1870, PUTNAM'S encouraged American writers from all sections of the country. The editors attacked HARPER'S MONTHLY for its reliance on English writers.

Putnam, George Haven. GEORGE PALMER PUTNAM: A MEMOIR. New York: G.P. Putnam's Sons, 1912.

Chapters IX and XVII review the history of PUTNAM'S.

Roper, Laura Wood. "Mr. Law and PUTNAM'S MONTHLY MAGAZINE: A Note on a Phase in the Career of Frederick Law Olmsted." AMERICAN LITERATURE, 26 (1954), 88-93.

Olmsted edited PUTNAM'S from 1855 approximately until the sale of the journal to EMERSON'S UNITED STATES MAGAZINE in 1856.

Tew, Arnold Gerard. "PUTNAM'S MAGAZINE: Its Men and Their Literary and Social Policies." Dissertation, Case Western Reserve University, 1969.

Tew surveys the magazine's publishing history and discusses its editors, contributors, and contents.

*   *   *   *   *

ST. NICHOLAS (1873-1940, 1943)

Dodge, Mary Mapes. "Children's Magazines." SCRIBNER'S MONTHLY, 6 (1873), 352-54.

The editor of the ST. NICHOLAS expresses her general views on what a children's magazine should do.

Saler, Elizabeth C., and Edwin H. Cady. "The ST. NICHOLAS and the Serious Artist." ESSAYS MOSTLY ON PERIODICAL PUBLISHING IN AMERICA. Ed. James Woodress. Durham, N.C.: Duke University Press, 1973. Pp. 162-70.

Although edited as a children's magazine, the ST. NICHOLAS published the work of important writers, and its pages even reflect the controversy over realism versus romanticism. It thus deserves more attention than it has been given.

*   *   *   *   *

SCRIBNER'S MAGAZINE (1887-1939)

Allen, Frederick Lewis. "Fifty Years of SCRIBNER'S MAGAZINE." SCRIBNER'S MAGAZINE, 101 (January 1937), 17-24.

Allen recounts the events which led to the establishment of SCRIBNER'S MAGAZINE, and then discusses the contents of its early issues.

*   *   *   *   *

SCRIBNER'S MONTHLY (1870-1881), later THE CENTURY ILLUSTRATED
MONTHLY MAGAZINE (1881-1929)

"The CENTURY Magazine 1870-1924." PAN-AMERICAN MAGAZINE, 37
(1924), 341-58.

> This is a sketch of the periodical's history.

"CENTURY'S Twentieth Anniversary." CENTURY, 41 (1890), 148.

> This is a general statement about the aims and accomplishments of
> the publication since its founding in 1870.

Clemens, Cyril. "An Unpublished Letter from James Lane Allen." AMERICAN
LITERATURE, 9 (1937), 355-56.

> In a letter of December 8, 1888, reprinted here, Allen pleads for
> higher payment from editor Gilder for his contributions to the CEN-
> TURY.

DeVinne, Theodore L. "The Printing of 'The Century.'" CENTURY, 41 (November 1890), 87-99.

> DeVinne, head of the firm that printed the CENTURY, describes
> in detail the production of the magazine, including the superior
> illustrations for which it was so well known.

"Forty Years of This Magazine: A Survey of the CENTURY's Progress in the
Arts of Illustration." CENTURY, 81 (1910), 131-50.

> A discussion of the periodical's technical excellence in the field
> of illustration is followed by a number of full-page illustrations
> showing the progress of the art in the CENTURY through the years.

FRUIT AMONG THE LEAVES: AN ANNIVERSARY ANTHOLOGY. Ed. Samuel
C. Chew. New York: Appleton-Century-Crofts, 1950.

> In an extensive introduction Chew relates in detail the histories of
> the Century Company's SCRIBNER'S MONTHLY (later the CEN-
> TURY) and ST. NICHOLAS (pp. 67-141). He examines the var-
> ious types of literature which appeared in these journals from the
> 1870's to their sale in 1930 to other firms.

Gilder, Richard Watson. LETTERS OF RICHARD WATSON GILDER. Ed. Rosa-
mond Gilder. Boston: Houghton, Mifflin, 1916.

> Chapter XI, "Editor and Author," includes letters which discuss
> editorial policy and other matters relating to SCRIBNER'S MONTH-
> LY.

Holland, J.G. "Topics of the Time: 'Scribner's Monthly.'--Historical."
SCRIBNER'S MONTHLY, 22 (1881), 302-3.

> This historical sketch focuses on SCRIBNER'S pioneer work in the
> art of illustration.

John, Arthur W. "A History of SCRIBNER'S MONTHLY and the CENTURY ILLUSTRATED MONTHLY MAGAZINE, 1870-1900." Dissertation, Harvard University, 1951.

Johnson, Robert Underwood. REMEMBERED YESTERDAYS. Boston: Little, Brown, 1923.

> Johnson worked for forty years on the publication, and after Gilder's death served as editor from 1909 to 1913. Chapter IV, "Forty Years of Editing: 1873-1913," covers the journal's various editors and their work, and Chapter VII, "Special Projects of the CENTURY," provides information on projects such as the Civil War series.

Murray, Marion Reid. "The 1870's in American Literature." AMERICAN SPEECH, 1 (1926), 323-28.

> Unlike its competitors, SCRIBNER'S "was rather intimately related to American literature" and "was in close touch with its varied tendencies and interests," including a concern for post-bellum southern literary talent.

Peckham, Harry Houston. JOSIAH GILBERT HOLLAND IN RELATION TO HIS TIMES. Philadelphia: University of Pennsylvania Press, 1940.

> Chapter VIII on "The Old SCRIBNER'S" relates the story of Holland's meeting in Europe with Roswell Smith and the consequent founding of SCRIBNER'S in 1870. The first ten years of the journal's history and its phenomenal success are also examined.

Pennell, Joseph. THE ADVENTURES OF AN ILLUSTRATOR: MOSTLY IN FOLLOWING HIS AUTHORS IN AMERICA & EUROPE. Boston: Little, Brown, 1925.

> In Chapter VI, "The First Commission for the CENTURY," Pennell discusses some of his work for the publication.

Plunkett, Mrs. H.M. JOSIAH GILBERT HOLLAND. New York: Charles Scribner's Sons, 1894.

> Chapters VII and VIII (pp. 68-98) cover the founding of SCRIBNER'S, Holland's work as editor, his contributions, the periodical's pioneer work in illustration, and an account of its nationwide success.

"A Retrospect of 'The Century.'" CENTURY, 81 (1910), 151-54.

> This commemorative article looks back at the publishing past, and then into the future.

Scott, Arthur L. "The CENTURY MAGAZINE Edits HUCKLEBERRY FINN, 1884-1885." AMERICAN LITERATURE, 27 (1955), 356-62.

> Editor Gilder deleted or changed a number of passages from the portions of Twain's novel which appeared in the CENTURY. Scott examines these alterations in order to gain "a ready insight into

the genteel culture of an era which ignored TOM SAWYER and abused HUCKLEBERRY FINN, while taking THE PRINCE AND THE PAUPER to its heart."

Sloane, David E.E. "Censoring for THE CENTURY MAGAZINE: R.W. Gilder to John Hay on THE BREAD-WINNERS, 1882-1884." AMERICAN LITERARY REALISM, 1870-1910, 4 (1971), 255-67.

Some of Gilder's editorial policies are revealed in the changes he made in THE BREAD-WINNERS before serializing it in the CENTURY.

Smith, Herbert Franklin. "The Editorial Influence of Richard Watson Gilder, 1870-1909." Dissertation, Rutgers University, 1961.

Gilder's constructive and liberal policies are emphasized in order to counterbalance unfair criticism of his editorship.

_____. "Joel Chandler Harris's Contributions to SCRIBNER'S MONTHLY and CENTURY MAGAZINE, 1880-1887." GEORGIA HISTORICAL QUARTERLY, 47 (1963), 169-79.

SCRIBNER'S was the first major journal to seek contributions from Harris, with the result that from 1880 to 1887 his work was almost all published there. Smith examines in detail the writer-editor relationship between Harris and Gilder.

_____. RICHARD WATSON GILDER. New York: Twayne, 1970.

This isn't so much a biography as a study of Gilder as editor for thirty-nine years of the CENTURY. Smith examines his editorial policies and critical ideas, and gives detailed accounts of his relationships with specific writers, including Twain, Whitman, and Garland.

Smith, Herbert F., and Michael Peinovich. "THE BOSTONIANS: Creation and Revision." BULLETIN OF THE NEW YORK PUBLIC LIBRARY, 73 (1969), 298-308.

THE BOSTONIANS first appeared as a thirteen-part serial in the CENTURY from 1884 to 1885, and became known in its business offices as a dull failure. This article in fact reprints a letter from editor Gilder informing James that the work was too long.

Tomsich, John. A GENTEEL ENDEAVOUR: AMERICAN CULTURE AND POLITICS IN THE GILDED AGE. Stanford, Calif.: Stanford University Press, 1971.

Gilder's political, social, and editorial ideas are discussed here.

Tooker, L. Frank. THE JOYS AND TRIBULATIONS OF AN EDITOR. New York: Century, 1924. This account was first published in a slightly shorter version, "As I Saw It from an Editor's Desk." CENTURY, 106 (1923), 723-33, 925-34; 107 (1923-1924), 129-40, 257-68, 428-36, 615-24, 748-57, 838-46; 108 (1924), 115-23, 260-71, 399-408, 536-47, 666-77, 828-40.

Tooker, former editor, relates anecdotes from his years on the CEN-
TURY, including stories of various personalities, relations between
editors and contributors, and office routine.

Wagenknecht, Edward. "Richard Watson Gilder: Poet and Editor of the Transi-
tion." BOSTON UNIVERSITY STUDIES IN ENGLISH, 1 (1955), 84–95.

Wagenknecht examines the values Gilder held as poet, reformer,
and editor of the CENTURY.

*   *   *   *   *

THE SPIRIT OF THE TIMES (1831–1861)

Betts, John Rickards. "Sporting Journalism in Nineteenth-Century America."
AMERICAN QUARTERLY, 5 (1953), 39–56.

THE SPIRIT OF THE TIMES is one of a number of periodicals discussed in this examination of American sports journalism.

Blair, Walter. NATIVE AMERICAN HUMOR. 2nd ed. San Francisco: Chandler Publishing Co., 1960.

Blair discusses the SPIRIT and its humorous literature of the old
Southwest on pp. 82–86.

Brigham, Clarence S. "Letter to the Editor." PAPERS OF THE BIBLIOGRA-
PHICAL SOCIETY OF AMERICA, 48 (1954), 300–301.

Brigham, director of the American Antiquarian Society, presents information on the early publishing history of the SPIRIT, which solves
some of the problems which Norris Yates encountered in his investigation of the journal (see below).

Collins, Carvel. "Bibliographic Notes." PAPERS OF THE BIBLIOGRAPHICAL
SOCIETY OF AMERICA, 40 (1946), 164–68.

The source of bibliographical confusion over this journal is caused
by the fact that three distinct SPIRITS were published in New York,
for a time simultaneously. The first SPIRIT OF THE TIMES, founded
by William T. Porter, ran from 1831 to 1861. Porter, along with
George Wilkes, also started PORTER'S SPIRIT OF THE TIMES in
1856, and this journal lasted until 1862. The third was WILKES'
SPIRIT OF THE TIMES, founded in 1859 and terminated in 1902.

_____. "An Extra Issue of the 'Spirit of the Times.'" PAPERS OF THE
BIBLIOGRAPHICAL SOCIETY OF AMERICA, 48 (1954), 198.

Collins describes the contents of a newly-discovered extra issue of
the SPIRIT dated May 10, 1842.

Current-Garcia, Eugene. "Alabama Writers in the SPIRIT." ALABAMA RE-
VIEW, 10 (1957), 243–69.

Alabama writers, notably Johnson Jones Hooper, the creator of

Simon Suggs, contributed humorous stories and sketches to this New
York magazine in the years before the Civil War.

_____. "'Mr. Spirit' and THE BIG BEAR OF ARKANSAS: A Note on the
Genesis of Southwestern Sporting and Humor Literature." AMERICAN LITERA-
TURE, 27 (1955), 332-46.

Through his work as anthologist and as editor of THE SPIRIT OF
THE TIMES, William T. Porter helped to establish an important tradition of humor and sporting literature.

_____. "'York's Tall Son' and His Southern Correspondents." AMERICAN
QUARTERLY, 7 (1955), 371-84.

Through its promotion of southern literature, the SPIRIT helped to
lay the groundwork for later writers such as Faulkner and Caldwell.
This article examines in detail the periodical's contents in the late
1840's and early 1850's.

Eberstadt, Lindley. "The Passing of a Noble 'Spirit.'" PAPERS OF THE BIB-
LIOGRAPHICAL SOCIETY OF AMERICA, 44 (1950), 372-73.

A newly-discovered eleventh and final volume of PORTER'S SPIRIT
is discussed. PORTER'S SPIRIT is the second of the three SPIRITS
differentiated in Collins' "Bibliographic Notes" (see above). Eberstadt reflects on the possible reasons for the death of PORTER'S
SPIRIT in 1861.

Hauck, Richard Boyd. "The Dickens Controversy in the SPIRIT OF THE TIMES."
PMLA, 85 (1970), 278-83.

Editor Porter pirated the work of English writers including Dickens,
but after adverse reaction from the public to Dickens' AMERICAN
NOTES, Porter dropped the Englishman and turned increasingly to
contributions from American writers.

_____. "The Literary Content of the New York SPIRIT OF THE TIMES 1831-
1856." Dissertation, University of Illinois, 1965.

Hauck analyzes the periodical's contents and Porter's editorial
policies.

_____. "Predicting a Native Literature: William T. Porter's First Issue of
the SPIRIT OF THE TIMES." MISSISSIPPI QUARTERLY, 22 (1968-1969), 77-
84.

Two editorials in the first issue of the SPIRIT, reprinted here in full,
reveal Porter's clear intention to foster realistic native literature, as
well as his surprisingly accurate estimate of future trends in American writing.

Houtchens, Lawrence H. "The SPIRIT OF THE TIMES and a 'New Work by
Boz.'" PMLA, 67 (1952), 94-100.

In order to take revenge on pirating periodicals, the SPIRIT pub-

lished a contribution supposedly by Dickens and watched rivals
steal the fake for their own pages.

McDermott, John Francis. "The SPIRIT OF THE TIMES Reviews MOBY DICK."
NEW ENGLAND QUARTERLY, 30 (1957), 392-95.

A December 6, 1851, review praised the novel highly.

TALL TALES OF THE SOUTHWEST: AN ANTHOLOGY OF SOUTHERN AND
SOUTHWESTERN HUMOR 1830-1860. Ed. Franklin J. Meine. New York:
Alfred A. Knopf, 1930.

Pp. xxvii-xxix of the "Introduction" discuss Porter and the SPIRIT.
Included is an "interpretive sketch" of the man and the publication
by associate editor George Wilkes, written at the time of Porter's
death.

Yates, Norris W. "Folksongs in the SPIRIT OF THE TIMES." SOUTHERN
FOLKLORE QUARTERLY, 26 (1962), 326-34.

Editor Porter published the lyrics of the folksongs sent by contributors in the South and Southwest, some of which are reprinted and
discussed here.

_____. "The SPIRIT OF THE TIMES: Its Early History and some of Its Contri-
butors." PAPERS OF THE BIBLIOGRAPHICAL SOCIETY OF AMERICA, 48
(1954), 117-48.

Yates investigates the publishing history of the magazine during its
early years, a phase of its career not previously examined.

_____. WILLIAM T. PORTER AND THE SPIRIT OF THE TIMES: A STUDY OF
THE BIG BEAR SCHOOL OF HUMOR. Baton Rouge: Louisiana State University Press, 1957.

This is a detailed and thorough investigation of the career of editor Porter, the publishing history and contents of the SPIRIT, and
the writers who contributed tales and sketches to it. The main
thesis is the SPIRIT's role in presenting the regional comic literature of the Southwest to a national readership.

*   *   *   *   *

THE TIME-PIECE AND LITERARY COMPANION (1797-1798)

Smith, Frank. "Philip Freneau and THE TIME-PIECE AND LITERARY COMPAN-
ION." AMERICAN LITERATURE, 4 (1932), 270-87.

Freneau edited this political and literary tri-weekly in 1797, and
his disappointment with its lack of success caused him never again
to attempt a similar journalistic venture.

*   *   *   *   *

TRUTH (1886-1906)

Linneman, William R. "Stephen Crane's Contributions to TRUTH." AMERICAN LITERATURE, 31 (1959), 196-97.

> Crane contributed two satires to the magazine in 1893 and 1894.

* * * * *

THE UNITED STATES MAGAZINE AND DEMOCRATIC REVIEW (1837-1859)

"The DEMOCRATIC REVIEW and O.A. Brownson." THE PRESENT, 1 (1843), 72.

> Probably written by William Henry Channing, this piece praises Brownson's work on the DEMOCRATIC REVIEW, and then hopes that his BOSTON QUARTERLY REVIEW will be started again because "it was the best journal this country ever produced."

Fuller, Landon E. "The UNITED STATES MAGAZINE AND DEMOCRATIC REVIEW, 1837-1859: A Study of Its History, Contents and Significance." Dissertation, University of North Carolina, 1948.

* * * * *

THE UNITED STATES REVIEW AND LITERARY GAZETTE (1826-1827)

Glicksberg, Charles I. "Bryant and the UNITED STATES REVIEW." NEW ENGLAND QUARTERLY, 7 (1934), 687-701.

> In October 1826, THE NEW-YORK REVIEW, AND ATHENEUM MAGAZINE, edited by William Cullen Bryant, merged with the UNITED STATES LITERARY GAZETTE, and the new journal was named THE UNITED STATES REVIEW AND LITERARY GAZETTE. Even though Bryant became the journal's New York editor, and plans for success included simultaneous publication in Boston and New York, the publication only survived for thirteen months.

* * * * *

VANITY FAIR (1859-1863)

Nardin, James T. "Civil War Humor: The War in VANITY FAIR." CIVIL WAR HISTORY, 2 (September 1956), 67-85.

> During its career from 1859 to 1863, this humor magazine attempted to dispel some of the gloom by joking about Civil War issues.

Seitz, Don C. ARTEMUS WARD: A BIOGRAPHY AND BIBLIOGRAPHY. New York: Harper and Brothers, 1919.

> Chapter IV, "New York--'Vanity Fair,'" covers Ward's association with the periodical, first as a contributor and then as an editor in 1861 and 1862. Chapter IX reprints "'Vanity Fair' Romances and Other Contributions."

* * * * *

THE YOUNG NEW YORKER (1878-1879)

Durham, Philip. "The Loyal Sons of America and THE YOUNG NEW YORK-ER." NEW YORK HISTORY, 38 (1957), 397-405.

In 1879 the publishing house of Beadle and Adams founded the nationalistic YOUNG NEW YORKER, a weekly publication for young people, hoping to provide an additional outlet for its dime novels.

Chapter 5

LITERARY PERIODICALS

OF THE SOUTH

Chapter 5

LITERARY PERIODICALS OF THE SOUTH

General Studies

Atchison, Ray Morris. "Southern Literary Magazines, 1865-1887." Dissertation, Duke University, 1956.

Brantley, Rabun Lee. GEORGIA JOURNALISM OF THE CIVIL WAR PERIOD. Nashville: George Peabody College for Teachers, 1929.

This study covers books as well as newspapers and other periodicals.

Calhoun, Richard James. "Literary Criticism in Southern Periodicals: 1828-1860." Dissertation, University of North Carolina, 1959.

Criticism in the following journals is examined: THE SOUTHERN REVIEW, THE SOUTHERN LITERARY MESSENGER, THE SOUTHERN LITERARY JOURNAL, THE MAGNOLIA, THE SOUTHERN QUARTERLY REVIEW, THE ORION, DEBOW'S REVIEW, THE SOUTHERN LITERARY GAZETTE, THE SOUTHERN AND WESTERN MONTHLY MAGAZINE AND REVIEW and RUSSELL'S MAGAZINE.

Cardwell, Guy A. "Charleston Periodicals, 1795-1860: A Study in Literary Influences, with a Descriptive Check List of Seventy-Five Magazines." Dissertation, University of North Carolina, 1936.

_____. "The Influence of Addison on Charleston Periodicals, 1795-1860." STUDIES IN PHILOLOGY, 35 (1938), 456-70.

Charleston serial publications, including "the literary essay periodicals" such as THE TRAITEUR, THE VIGIL, and THE QUIVER, were greatly influenced by the writing style of the Age of Anne long after the vogue had passed in the North.

_____. "THE QUIVER and THE FLORAL WREATH: Two Rare Charleston Periodicals." NORTH CAROLINA HISTORICAL REVIEW, 16 (1939), 418-27.

Cardwell states that "the discovery of a complete file of THE QUI-

VER and of excerpts from THE FLORAL WREATH AND LADIES'
MONTHLY MAGAZINE adds measurably to our understanding of
literary activities in a magazine-publishing center of the Old
South."

Cohen, Sidney J. THREE NOTABLE ANTE-BELLUM MAGAZINES OF SOUTH
CAROLINA. Columbia: University of South Carolina Press, 1915.

> Cohen discusses RUSSELL'S, THE MAGNOLIA and THE SOUTHERN
> LITERARY MESSENGER.

Cotterill, R.S. THE OLD SOUTH: THE GEOGRAPHIC, ECONOMIC, SOCIAL,
POLITICAL, AND CULTURAL EXPANSION, INSTITUTIONS, AND NATIONAL-
ISM OF THE ANTE-BELLUM SOUTH. Glendale, Calif.: Arthur H. Clark,
1937.

> Pp. 299-304 briefly discuss various literary periodicals published in
> the South before the Civil War.

Ellison, Rhoda Coleman. EARLY ALABAMA PUBLICATIONS: A STUDY IN
LITERARY INTERESTS. University, Ala.: University of Alabama Press, 1947.

> Chapter III, "Literary Interests Reflected in Periodicals," examines
> the policies and contents of numerous short-lived periodicals ap-
> pearing up to 1870.

Flanders, Bertram Holland. EARLY GEORGIA MAGAZINES: LITERARY PERIOD-
ICALS TO 1865. Athens: University of Georgia Press, 1944.

> Flanders' book reveals a surprisingly large number of literary period-
> icals founded in the state during this time, almost all of them
> obscure and now forgotten. The work concludes with thorough ap-
> pendices giving details on the contributors as well as on the period-
> icals themselves. It began as Flanders' dissertation at Duke,
> finished in 1942.

Flanders, Ralph B. "Newspapers and Periodicals in the Washington Memorial
Library, Macon, Georgia." NORTH CAROLINA HISTORICAL REVIEW, 7
(1930), 220-23.

> On p. 223 Flanders briefly discusses publisher C.R. Hanleiter's two
> literary journals of the late 1830's and early 1840's, THE SOUTH-
> ERN POST AND LITERARY ASPIRANT and THE SOUTHERN MISCEL-
> LANY.

French, John C. "Poe's Literary Baltimore." MARYLAND HISTORICAL MAG-
AZINE, 32 (1937), 101-12.

> French examines the literary activities in Baltimore from 1831 to
> 1835, the period of Poe's residence in the city. He discusses THE
> BALTIMORE SATURDAY VISITER, a magazine which awarded Poe a

fifty-dollar literary prize for "Ms. Found in a Bottle."

Gilmer, Gertrude. "A Critique of Certain Georgia Ante Bellum Literary Magazines Arranged Chronologically, and a Checklist." GEORGIA HISTORICAL QUARTERLY, 18 (1934), 293-334.

> The publishing and editorial histories of some little-known periodicals are examined here.

Guilds, John C., Jr. "William Gilmore Simms as a Magazine Editor, 1825-1845: With Special Reference to His Contributions." Dissertation, Duke University, 1954.

> Simms' work on various periodicals is studied here.

Herbert, Edward Thomas. "William Gilmore Simms as Editor and Literary Critic." Dissertation, University of Wisconsin, 1958.

> The first chapter covers Simms' editorial career.

Hoole, William Stanley. "William Gilmore Simms's Career as Editor." GEORGIA HISTORICAL QUARTERLY, 19 (1935), 47-54.

> This article surveys Simms' work on various periodicals, emphasizing his allegiance to the culture of his region.

Hubbell, Jay B. THE SOUTH IN AMERICAN LITERATURE, 1607-1900. Durham, N.C.: Duke University Press, 1954.

> The following sections of Hubbell's study deal with literary journals: "Newspapers and Magazines" from 1789-1830 (pp. 218-19); "Southern Magazines" from 1830-1865 (pp. 366-69); "Southern Magazines" and "Southern Writers and Northern Magazines" after the Civil War (pp. 716-33). Although brief, these discussions contain much information on the contents and policies of the magazines.

_____. "Southern Magazines." CULTURE IN THE SOUTH. Ed. W.T. Couch. Chapel Hill: University of North Carolina Press, 1934. Pp. 158-82.

> The history of southern literary journals is surveyed, from early periodicals such as RUSSELL'S and THE SOUTHERN LITERARY MESSENGER to modern ones, including THE VIRGINIA QUARTERLY REVIEW.

Huff, Lawrence. "The Literary Publications of Joseph Addison Turner." GEORGIA HISTORICAL QUARTERLY, 46 (1962), 223-36.

> Turner, a Georgia planter who engaged in a variety of literary pursuits, founded a number of periodicals from the late 1840's through the mid-1860's, including TURNER'S MONTHLY in 1848

and the PLANTATION in 1860. His most successful journal was
THE COUNTRYMAN, which lasted from 1862 to 1866.

Ingle, Edward. "Two Southern Magazines." PUBLICATIONS OF THE SOUTH-
ERN HISTORY ASSOCIATION, 1 (1897), 45-52.

Ingle discusses the history and contents of THE SOUTHERN LITER-
ARY MESSENGER and DEBOW'S COMMERCIAL REVIEW OF THE
SOUTH AND WEST.

McLean, Frank. "Periodicals Published in the South Before 1800." Dissertation, University of Virginia, 1928.

This study includes an annotated bibliography.

Mims, Edwin. "Southern Magazines." THE SOUTH IN THE BUILDING OF
THE NATION. Richmond: Southern Historical Publication Society, 1909. VII,
437-69.

Mims views the careers of a number of literary periodicals published in the South in the nineteenth century, and concludes that although almost all were short-lived, their ambition is commendable.

Moore, Rayburn S. "Southern Writers and Northern Literary Magazines, 1865-
1890." Dissertation, Duke University, 1956.

Moore discusses the contributions of southern writers and how they
were received by northern editors.

Riley, Susan B. "The Hazards of Periodical Publishing in the South During the
Nineteenth Century." TENNESSEE HISTORICAL QUARTERLY, 21 (1962), 365-
76.

Although there was no shortage of ambitious editors, the southern
public failed to support their ventures, and consequently most literary periodicals were short lived. Both obscure and well-known
publications are discussed.

_____. "The Southern Literary Magazine of the Mid-Nineteenth Century."
TENNESSEE HISTORICAL QUARTERLY, 23 (1964), 221-36.

Southern periodicals struggled for survival, unsuccessfully for the
most part, against public apathy and lack of patronage. Their
plight reveals much about the intellectual milieu of the section
during this period.

Rogers, Edward Reinhold. FOUR SOUTHERN MAGAZINES. Charlottesville:
University of Virginia, 1902.

Rogers briefly examines THE SOUTHERN LITERARY MESSENGER,
DEBOW'S REVIEW, and two Charleston periodicals. This was Rogers'

dissertation, completed in the same year.

Simms, William Gilmore. THE LETTERS OF WILLIAM GILMORE SIMMS. Eds. Mary C. Simms Oliphant, Alfred Taylor Odell and T.C. Duncan Eaves. 5 vols. Columbia, S.C.: University of South Carolina Press, 1952.

> Simms' letters refer to his various involvements with literary journals.

Stearns, Bertha M. "Southern Magazines for Ladies (1819-1860)." SOUTH ATLANTIC QUARTERLY, 31 (1932), 70-87.

> The writer discusses briefly a number of periodicals, most of them literary. The brevity of critical examination causes the article to resemble a heavily-annotated bibliography.

Terwilliger, W. Bird. "A History of Literary Periodicals in Baltimore." Dissertation, University of Maryland, 1941.

Trent, William P. WILLIAM GILMORE SIMMS. 1892; rpt. New York: Greenwood Press, 1969.

> Simms' involvement with southern journals is discussed here.

Uhler, John Earle. "Literary Taste and Culture in Baltimore: A Study of the Periodical Literature of Baltimore from 1815 to 1833." Dissertation, Johns Hopkins University, 1927.

Wish, Harvey. "George Frederick Holmes and Southern Periodical Literature of the Mid-Nineteenth Century." JOURNAL OF SOUTHERN HISTORY, 7 (1941), 343-56.

> This Virginia writer has been largely forgotten because his work appeared in short-lived southern periodicals which are now forgotten. During his career he was assistant editor under Simms of THE SOUTHERN LITERARY MESSENGER and a close friend of Simms' successor, Benjamin Blake Minor.

Studies of Individual Periodicals

THE ALBUM (1825)

Guilds, John C., Jr. "Simms's First Magazine: THE ALBUM." STUDIES IN BIBLIOGRAPHY, 8 (1956), 169-83.

> Simms' first editorial position in 1825 offered him valuable training for his future career as editor and author. Guilds evaluates his work on this short-lived Charleston periodical and includes an appendix of Simms' contributions.

* * * * * *

THE ARKANSAW TRAVELER (1882-1916)

Linneman, William R. "Opie Read and THE ARKANSAW TRAVELER: The Trials of a Regional Humor Magazine." MIDWEST FOLKLORE, 10 (Spring 1960), 5-10.

> This article covers the publishing history and contents of the TRA-VELER from its founding in 1882, through its move to Chicago in 1887, to 1893 when Read relinquished his editorship and the journal became less literary and more strictly comic.

* * * * *

THE BALTIMORE SATURDAY VISITER (1832-1850)

French, John C. "Poe and the BALTIMORE SATURDAY VISITER." MODERN LANGUAGE NOTES, 33 (1918), 257-67.

> Poe was "rescued from obscurity" in 1833 when he won a short story prize offered by this literary weekly. French also discovers some previously unknown poems published in it by Poe.

* * * * *

THE BUGLE-HORN OF LIBERTY (1863)

Flanders, Bertram H. "BUGLE-HORN OF LIBERTY: A Confederate Humorous Magazine." EMORY UNIVERSITY QUARTERLY, 9 (1953), 79-85.

> Flanders examines the magazine's publishing history and contents.

* * * * *

THE CHARLESTON SPECTATOR, AND LADIES' LITERARY PORT FOLIO (1806)

Cardwell, Guy A., Jr. "A Newly-Discovered Charleston Periodical." AMER-ICAN LITERATURE, 14 (1942), 306-8.

> "Like serials which preceded it (particularly the TRAITEUR and the VIGIL), it follows closely in the tradition of the TATLER and the SPECTATOR."

* * * * *

THE COSMOPOLITAN: AN OCCASIONAL (1833)

Guilds, John C. "William Gilmore Simms and the COSMOPOLITAN." GEOR-GIA HISTORICAL QUARTERLY, 41 (1957), 31-41.

> One of three editors of this short-lived Charleston journal, Simms received through his contributions to its pages valuable training as a short story writer and novelist.

* * * * *

THE COUNTRYMAN (1861-1865)

Cousins, Paul M. JOEL CHANDLER HARRIS: A BIOGRAPHY. Baton Rouge: Louisiana State University Press, 1968.

> Chapter IV, "Prologue to a Literary Career," offers information on Joseph Addison Turner's COUNTRYMAN, a periodical with which Harris was associated.

* * * * *

THE FAMILY COMPANION AND LADIES' MIRROR (1841-1843)

Rees, Robert A., and Marjorie Griffin. "Index and Author Guide to the FAMILY COMPANION (1841-1843)." STUDIES IN BIBLIOGRAPHY, 25 (1972), 205-12.

> This list covers the entire career of the short-lived COMPANION, and is preceded by a general discussion of its major contributors and history.

_____. "William Gilmore Simms and THE FAMILY COMPANION." STUDIES IN BIBLIOGRAPHY, 24 (1971), 109-29.

> Simms' letters of editorial advice to Benjamin F. and Sarah Lawrence Griffin, editors of the COMPANION, are reprinted in full. His interest in the Macon, Georgia, literary venture lasted throughout 1841, and although he offered encouragement, he was, as a result of his own personal editorial experiences, at times skeptical of the journal's possibilities for success.

* * * * *

THE LAND WE LOVE (1866-1869)

Atchison, Ray M. "THE LAND WE LOVE: a Southern Post-Bellum Magazine of Agriculture, Literature, and Literary History." NORTH CAROLINA HISTORICAL REVIEW 37 (1960), 506-15.

> Founded in Charlotte, North Carolina, in 1866 by General Daniel Harvey Hill, THE LAND WE LOVE was the first journal to publish battle accounts by Confederate officers, and also was an early advocate of reconciliation. Atchison considers its fiction and literary criticism to be generally weak.

* * * * *

THE MAGNOLIA (1841-1843)

Guilds, John C. "Simms as Editor and Prophet: The Flowering and Early Death of the Southern MAGNOLIA." SOUTHERN LITERARY JOURNAL, 4 (Spring 1972), 69-72.

> Simms became first a contributor, then associate editor, and finally

editor of the journal, a position he held from July 1842 until close to the magazine's collapse in June 1843. Guilds discusses THE MAGNOLIA's changes of location, changes of title, and the quality of its literature, which he feels to have been among the best in the South.

* * * * *

THE MINERVA AND EMERALD (1830?)

Starrett, Vincent. "A Poe Mystery Uncovered: The Last MINERVA Review of Al Aaraaf." SATURDAY REVIEW OF LITERATURE, May 1, 1943, pp. 4-5, 25.

John Hill Hewitt, editor of the now obscure Baltimore weekly and himself a poet, published a severely critical review of Poe's work in the MINERVA, the date of which is unknown.

* * * * *

THE ORION (1842-1844)

Abney, Beth. "The ORION as a Literary Publication." GEORGIA HISTORICAL QUARTERLY, 48 (1964), 411-24.

This article discusses the contents of THE ORION during its short career, and relates its history to the general history of ante-bellum southern literary periodicals.

* * * * *

OUR LIVING AND OUR DEAD (1873-1876)

Atchison, Ray M. "OUR LIVING AND OUR DEAD: A Post-Bellum North Carolina Magazine of Literature and History." NORTH CAROLINA HISTORICAL REVIEW, 40 (1963), 423-33.

During the magazine's career editor Stephen D. Pool strove to record historically the role that his state and its soldiers played in the Civil War. The literary sections of the publication include many of the critical views of native author Theodore Bryant Kingsbury.

* * * * *

THE PORTICO (1816-1818)

Fishwick, Marshall W. "THE PORTICO and Literary Nationalism After the War of 1812." WILLIAM AND MARY QUARTERLY, 8 (1951), 238-45.

THE PORTICO, published from 1816 to 1818, pioneered the movement for native American literature.

McCloskey, John C. "A Note on the PORTICO." AMERICAN LITERATURE, 8 (1936), 300-304.

McCloskey feels that the important role of THE PORTICO in the quest for an independent American literature, especially under the nationalistic editor Stephen Simpson, has been overlooked by critics and historians.

* * * * *

RUSSELL'S MAGAZINE (1857-1860)

Becker, Kate Harbes. PAUL HAMILTON HAYNE: LIFE AND LETTERS. Belmont, N.C.: Outline Co., 1951.

Chapter V covers "RUSSELL'S MAGAZINE," its contents and policies. Becker includes some of Hayne's correspondence to Richard Henry Stoddard and John Esten Cooke concerning the periodical.

Calhoun, Richard J. "The Ante-Bellum Literary Twilight: RUSSELL'S MAGAZINE." THE SOUTHERN LITERARY JOURNAL, 3 (Fall 1970), 89-110.

Calhoun sketches the three-year history of the journal, Hayne's prominent role in it, the reasons for its failure, and its similarities to and differences from other southern literary serials.

Dedmond, Francis B. "Editor Hayne to Editor Kingsbury: Three Significant Unpublished Letters." NORTH CAROLINA HISTORICAL REVIEW, 32 (1955), 92-101.

Hayne corresponded with and encouraged North Carolina journalist Theodore Bryant Kingsbury, who in the late 1850's was editing the weekly LEISURE HOUR: A LITERARY AND FAMILY NEWS JOURNAL.

Hayne, Paul Hamilton. "Ante-Bellum Charleston." THE SOUTHERN BIVOUAC, NS 1 (1885), 327-36.

Hayne reminisces about the founding of RUSSELL'S and his acquaintance with some of the contributors.

_____. A COLLECTION OF HAYNE LETTERS. Ed. Daniel Morley McKeithan. Austin: University of Texas Press, 1944.

This collection includes no index, but does contain letters in which Hayne discusses his editorship of RUSSELL'S.

Kennedy, Fronde. "Russell's Magazine." SOUTH ATLANTIC QUARTERLY, 18 (1919), 125-44.

Kennedy discusses the journal's founding by a Charleston group including William Gilmore Simms, publisher John Russell, and editor Hayne. He also covers the periodical's reception and its short history.

Long, Edgar. "RUSSELL'S MAGAZINE as an Expression of Ante-Bellum South Carolina Culture." Dissertation, University of South Carolina, 1932.

Vandiver, Frank E. "The Authorship of Certain Contributions to RUSSELL'S MAGAZINE." GEORGIA HISTORICAL QUARTERLY, 31 (1947), 118-20.

Vandiver ascertains the authorship of a series of travel letters which appeared in RUSSELL'S during its last two years of publication.

* * * * *

SCOTT'S MONTHLY MAGAZINE (1865-1869)

Atchison, Ray M. "SCOTT'S MONTHLY MAGAZINE: A Georgia Post-Bellum Periodical of Literature and Military History." GEORGIA HISTORICAL QUARTERLY, 49 (1965), 294-305.

SCOTT'S MONTHLY, published in Atlanta, was the first southern literary and historical journal to appear after the Civil War.

* * * * *

THE SOUTHERN BIVOUAC (1882-1887)

McKeithan, Daniel M. "Paul Hamilton Hayne and THE SOUTHERN BIVOUAC." UNIVERSITY OF TEXAS STUDIES IN ENGLISH, 17 (1937), 112-23.

Four essays which appeared in the BIVOUAC by Paul Hamilton Hayne, the periodical's chief contributor, are summarized here.

Moore, Rayburn S. "'A Distinctly Southern Magazine': The SOUTHERN BI-VOUAC." SOUTHERN LITERARY JOURNAL, 2 (Spring 1970), 51-65.

The journal's publishing history, contents, and contributors are examined. Founded in Louisville in 1882 to present Civil War history and southern literature, the BIVOUAC was eventually absorbed by the CENTURY in 1887.

* * * * *

THE SOUTHERN ILLUSTRATED NEWS (1862-1865)

Harwell, Richard Barksdale. "A Confederate View of the Southern Poets." AMERICAN LITERATURE, 24 (1952), 51-61.

Harwell discusses the policies and contents of the NEWS, a Richmond Civil War literary journal. Paul Hamilton Hayne's poem "The Southern Lyre" is reprinted from the magazine.

* * * * *

THE SOUTHERN LITERARY GAZETTE (Athens, Georgia) (1848-1849)

Jackson, David K. "Letters of Georgia Editors and a Correspondent." GEORGIA HISTORICAL QUARTERLY, 23 (1939), 170-76.

Correspondence primarily between an editor and contributor to the GAZETTE, published in Athens in 1848 and 1849, "reveals that

the struggle of literary journalists in Georgia in ante-bellum days
was much the same as in other parts of the South."

*   *   *   *   *

THE SOUTHERN LITERARY GAZETTE (Charleston, South Carolina) (1828-1829)

Guilds, John C.   "The 'Lost' Number of the SOUTHERN LITERARY GAZETTE."
STUDIES IN BIBLIOGRAPHY, 22 (1969), 266-73.

Guilds examines the contents of a recently-discovered issue of the
GAZETTE for November 1, 1829, ascertaining the authorship of
certain contributions by editor William Gilmore Simms.

_____.   "William Gilmore Simms and the SOUTHERN LITERARY GAZETTE."
STUDIES IN BIBLIOGRAPHY, 21 (1968), 59-92.

In the interim between his involvement with THE ALBUM and THE
COSMOPOLITAN, Simms edited this short-lived Charleston journal.   Guilds includes an appendix of Simms' contributions to the
journal.

*   *   *   *   *

THE SOUTHERN LITERARY MESSENGER (1834-1864) (Also see Appendix B)

Hughes, Robert M.   "Inaccurate Numerations in the SOUTHERN LITERARY
MESSENGER."   WILLIAM AND MARY COLLEGE QUARTERLY HISTORICAL
MAGAZINE, 9 (1929), 217.

Hughes reveals the errors, discusses why they were made, and sug-
gests renumerations.

Jackson, David K.   THE CONTRIBUTORS AND CONTRIBUTIONS TO THE
SOUTHERN LITERARY MESSENGER (1834-1864).   Charlottesville, Va.:   Historical Publishing Co., 1936.

The contents of every volume in the periodical's history are listed
in this thorough study, and the publication's "Prospectus" is reprinted in full.

_____.   "An Estimate of the Influence of THE SOUTHERN LITERARY MESSEN-
GER, 1834-1864."   THE SOUTHERN LITERARY MESSENGER, NS 1 (1939), 508-
14.

_____.   "Some Unpublished Letters of T.W. White to Lucian Minor."   TYLER'S
QUARTERLY HISTORICAL AND GENEALOGICAL MAGAZINE, 17 (1936), 224-
43; 18 (1936), 32-49.

White was founder and publisher of the MESSENGER, and these
letters written from 1835 to 1842 to a man who would later become
editor give information on the periodical and its contributors.

Jacobs, Robert D.   "Campaign for a Southern Literature: the SOUTHERN LIT-

ERARY MESSENGER." THE SOUTHERN LITERARY JOURNAL, 2 (Fall 1969), 66-98.

> From its founding to its disappearance during the Civil War, the MESSENGER promoted southern writers and attempted to awaken its public to the value of literature.

King, Joseph Leonard, Jr. DR. GEORGE WILLIAM BAGBY: A STUDY OF VIRGINIAN LITERATURE: 1850-1880. New York: Columbia University Press, 1927.

> In chapters V and VI, "Richmond: Literature and War" and "Richmond: Behind the Lines," Bagby's editorship of the MESSENGER during the Civil War is viewed in the light of its historical milieu.

Minor, Benjamin Blake. THE SOUTHERN LITERARY MESSENGER, 1834-1864. New York: Neale Publishing Co., 1905.

> This is an early study of the periodical's contents and publishing history.

Tucker, Edward L. "'A Rash and Perilous Enterprise': THE SOUTHERN LITERARY MESSENGER and the Men Who Made It." VIRGINIA CAVALCADE, 21 (Summer 1971), 14-21.

> A sketch of the journal's history is accompanied by portraits of the editors and illustrations from its pages.

Watts, Charles H., II. "Poe, Irving, and THE SOUTHERN LITERARY MESSENGER." AMERICAN LITERATURE, 27 (1955), 249-51.

> A previously unpublished letter from Poe to Irving dated June 7, 1836, requests a contribution for the MESSENGER.

* * * * *

THE SOUTHERN MISCELLANY (1842-1844)

Ellison, George R. "William Tappan Thompson and the SOUTHERN MISCELLANY, 1842-1844." MISSISSIPPI QUARTERLY, 23 (1969-1970), 155-68.

> Thompson founded the weekly MISCELLANY in Madison, Georgia, and for two years he and his contributors wrote humorous literature for its pages. A bibliography of contributions to the journal other than those of Thompson is included.

* * * * *

SOUTHERN PUNCH (1863-1865)

Linneman, William R. "SOUTHERN PUNCH: A Draught of Confederate Wit." SOUTHERN FOLKLORE QUARTERLY, 26 (1962), 131-36.

> Published in Richmond during the Civil War, this comic weekly attempted to spread wit and humor amid the general gloom.

* * * * *

THE SOUTHERN REVIEW (1828-1832)

Rhea, Linda. HUGH SWINTON LEGARE: A CHARLESTON INTELLECTUAL. Chapel Hill: University of North Carolina Press, 1934.

Chapter V is a survey of "THE SOUTHERN REVIEW and Other Southern Magazines," and Chapter VI covers the "SOUTHERN REVIEW: Contents." Legare edited and wrote for the journal throughout its four-year existence.

Welsh, John R. "An Early Pioneer: Legare's SOUTHERN REVIEW." THE SOUTHERN LITERARY JOURNAL, 3 (Spring 1971), 79-97.

Legare almost single-handedly ran the journal throughout its career, including providing most of its contents. Highly intellectual to the point of being pedantic, and unsympathetic to American literature, the periodical early ran into financial trouble and lacked public support.

*　　*　　*　　*　　*

THE SOUTHERN REVIEW (1867-1879)

Bennet, John Boyce. "Albert Taylor Bledsoe: Social and Religious Controversialist of the Old South." Dissertation, Duke University, 1942.

Bledsoe edited the REVIEW.

*　　*　　*　　*　　*

THE SOUTHERN ROSE (1832-1839)

Hoole, William Stanley. "The Gilmans and the SOUTHERN ROSE." NORTH CAROLINA HISTORICAL REVIEW, 11 (1934), 116-28.

Hoole discusses the history of this periodical, focusing on the activities of editor Caroline Gilman and her husband Dr. Samuel Gilman, minister and author.

Kennedy, Fronde. "The SOUTHERN ROSE-BUD and the SOUTHERN ROSE." SOUTH ATLANTIC QUARTERLY, 23 (1924), 10-19.

Kennedy traces the Charleston periodical's numerous changes in format, policy, and title following its establishment in 1832.

*　　*　　*　　*　　*

THE SUNNY SOUTH (1875-1907)

Moore, L. Hugh, Jr. "THE SUNNY SOUTH and Its Literature." GEORGIA REVIEW, 19 (1965), 176-85.

This article examines the contents of THE SUNNY SOUTH, an Atlanta periodical that achieved a circulation of over 100,000.

*　　*　　*　　*　　*

THE VIRGINIA LITERARY AND EVANGELICAL MAGAZINE (1818-1828)

Morrison, Alfred J. "The VIRGINIA LITERARY AND EVANGELICAL MAGA-
ZINE, Richmond, 1818-1828." WILLIAM AND MARY QUARTERLY, 19 (1911),
266-72.

> This religious periodical, seen here as the precursor in Richmond of
> THE SOUTHERN LITERARY MESSENGER, had as a major aim the
> discovery of local literary talent.

* * * * *

THE VIRGINIA LITERARY MUSEUM (1829-1830)

Wayland, John Walter. "THE VIRGINIA LITERARY MUSEUM." PUBLICATIONS
OF THE SOUTHERN HISTORY ASSOCIATION, 6 (1902), 1-14.

> Published weekly from June 1829 to June 1830, the MUSEUM was
> the first periodical founded by the University of Virginia.

Chapter 6

LITERARY PERIODICALS OF THE WEST

Chapter 6

LITERARY PERIODICALS OF THE WEST

General Studies

Andrews, Clarence A. A LITERARY HISTORY OF IOWA. Iowa City: University of Iowa Press, 1972.

> THE MIDLAND MONTHLY is one of the literary journals discussed in Chapter XIV, "Historians, Editors, and Publishers."

Bonk, W.J. "Periodical Publishing in Michigan Territory." BOOKS IN AMERICA'S PAST: ESSAYS HONORING RUDOLPH H. GJELSNESS. Ed. David Kaser. Charlottesville: University of Virginia Press, 1966. Pp. 86-104.

> Among the periodicals of various types examined are three extant literary journals, including THE HERALD OF LITERATURE AND SCIENCE.

Doepke, Dale Kay. "St. Louis Magazines Before the Civil War, 1832-1860." Dissertation, Washington University at St. Louis, 1963.

> The literary ideas and contents of these periodicals are discussed, and a bibliography is included.

Duffey, Bernard. THE CHICAGO RENAISSANCE IN AMERICAN LETTERS. 1956; rpt. Westport, Conn.: Greenwood Press, 1972.

> Pp. 66-73 discuss Francis Fisher Browne and the Chicago DIAL, and Stone and Kimball's little magazine of the 1890's, THE CHAPBOOK.

Duncan, Hugh Dalziel. THE RISE OF CHICAGO AS A LITERARY CENTER FROM 1885 TO 1920: A SOCIOLOGICAL ESSAY IN AMERICAN CULTURE. Totowa, N.J.: Bedminster Press, 1964.

> Chapter IV, "The Chicago Periodical Press," covers various literary journals which were founded after the Civil War, including THE LAKESIDE MONTHLY.

Flanagan, John T. "Early Literary Periodicals in Minnesota." MINNESOTA HISTORY, 26 (1945), 293-311.

> Flanagan discusses the editors and the contents of such journals as THE LITERARY NORTHWEST and THE BELLMAN.

_____. JAMES HALL: LITERARY PIONEER OF THE OHIO VALLEY. Minneapolis: University of Minnesota Press, 1941.

> Chapters entitled "Politician and Editor" and "Editor and Banker" relate the founding of two literary journals by Hall, THE ILLINOIS MONTHLY MAGAZINE in 1830 in Vandalia and THE WESTERN MONTHLY MAGAZINE in 1833 in Cincinnati.

_____. "Some Middlewestern Literary Magazines." PAPERS ON LANGUAGE AND LITERATURE, 3 (1967), 237-57.

> This study deals in summary fashion with periodicals before and after 1900, many of them little-known today. Among the more prominent discussed are THE LAKESIDE MONTHLY, THE DIAL, and THE CHAP-BOOK in Chicago, and REEDY'S MIRROR in St. Louis.

Fleming, Herbert E. MAGAZINES OF A MARKET-METROPOLIS: BEING A HISTORY OF THE LITERARY PERIODICALS AND LITERARY INTERESTS OF CHICAGO. Chicago: University of Chicago Press, 1906. This study first appeared in the AMERICAN JOURNAL OF SOCIOLOGY, 11 (1905), 377-403, 499-531, 784-816; 12 (1906), 68-118.

> This detailed study examines major and minor periodicals of Chicago which appeared throughout the nineteenth century. Fleming approaches his subject from a sociological viewpoint, emphasizing the milieu in which the periodicals struggled. The most important magazines examined are THE WESTERN MONTHLY, later called THE LAKESIDE MONTHLY, and THE DIAL.

Hounchell, Saul. "The Principal Literary Magazines of the Ohio Valley to 1840." Dissertation, Peabody, 1934.

Mendenhall, Lawrence. "Early Literature of the Miami Valley." THE MIDLAND MONTHLY, 8 (1897), 144-51.

> A number of early periodicals are touched upon in this article, including THE LITERARY CADET and LITERARY GAZETTE, both from Cincinnati in the 1820's, James Hall's WESTERN MONTHLY from the same city in the 1830's, and THE WESTERN MESSENGER.

Monaghan, Jay. "Literary Opportunities in Pioneer Times." JOURNAL OF THE ILLINOIS STATE HISTORICAL SOCIETY, 33 (1940), 412-37.

> Monaghan discusses various early western literary journals.

Payne, William Morton. "Literary Chicago." NEW ENGLAND MAGAZINE, NS 7 (1893), 683-700.

> This article, with numerous photos, covers literary activities in general, but a good portion of it focuses on the major periodicals of the city, especially THE WESTERN MONTHLY, later THE LAKE-SIDE MONTHLY.

Rusk, Ralph Leslie. THE LITERATURE OF THE MIDDLE WESTERN FRONTIER. 2 vols. New York: Columbia University Press, 1926.

> This study provides useful background information for a study of western literary magazines, but in addition Chapter III specifically covers "Newspapers and Magazines," and presents material on numerous little-known periodicals of the Midwest in the first half of the nineteenth century.

Severance, Frank H. "The Periodical Press of Buffalo, 1811-1915." BUFFALO HISTORICAL SOCIETY PUBLICATIONS, 19 (1915), 177-312.

> Although this essay and bibliography cover periodicals of all kinds, they do include some obscure literary journals. Much information on contents, editors, and publishing history of these journals is presented in annotations.

Stearns, Bertha Monica. "Early Western Magazines for Ladies." MISSISSIPPI VALLEY HISTORICAL REVIEW, 18 (1931), 319-30.

> Numerous ladies' literary magazines appeared in the area from western Pennsylvania to Kentucky throughout the early and middle years of the nineteenth century.

Taaue, James A. "William D. Gallagher, Champion of Western Literary Periodicals." OHIO HISTORICAL QUARTERLY, 69 (1960), 257-71.

> Among Gallagher's editorial ventures in the 1830's and 1840's were the CINCINNATI MIRROR, THE WESTERN MONTHLY and THE HESPERIAN, all of which had merit but failed to gain popular support.

Venable, W.H. BEGINNINGS OF LITERARY CULTURE IN THE OHIO VALLEY. 1891; rpt. New York: Peter Smith, 1949.

> This is an anecdotal study resulting from bibliographical work Venable had been doing. However Chapter III, "Early Periodical Literature of the Ohio Valley," is a thorough, detailed examination of a number of journals, some of them obscure, published in the first half of the nineteenth century. A "Partial List of Literary Periodicals Published in the Ohio Valley from the Year 1803 to 1860" is also included.

_____. "Early Periodical Literature of the Ohio Valley." MAGAZINE OF

WESTERN HISTORY, 8 (1888), 101-10, 197-203, 298-308, 459-65, 522-28; 9
(1888), 35-40.

> Venable relates in separate sections the histories of the following
> literary magazines: THE WESTERN REVIEW AND MISCELLANEOUS
> MAGAZINE, the Cincinnati LITERARY GAZETTE, James Hall's
> WESTERN MONTHLY MAGAZINE, THE WESTERN MESSENGER,
> MOORE'S WESTERN LADY'S BOOK, THE PARLOR MAGAZINE,
> THE QUARTERLY JOURNAL AND REVIEW, THE HERALD OF TRUTH,
> THE WESTERN QUARTERLY REVIEW, THE LADIES' REPOSITORY AND
> GATHERINGS OF THE WEST, THE GENIUS OF THE WEST, and the
> Cincinnati DIAL.

_____. "William Davis Gallagher." OHIO ARCHAEOLOGICAL AND HIS-
TORICAL QUARTERLY, 1 (1888), 358-75; 2 (1888), 309-26.

> Venable sketches the life of an Ohio journalist who founded and
> edited a number of literary periodicals in the 1830's and 1840's.
> He discusses the contents and publishing history of these journals,
> which include the CINCINNATI MIRROR and THE HESPERIAN.

Walker, Franklin. SAN FRANCISCO'S LITERARY FRONTIER. New York:
Alfred A. Knopf, 1939.

> Chapter V covers the history of "The 'Golden Era,'" and Chapter
> X that of "The 'Overland Monthly.'" Walker also examines
> THE HESPERIAN and THE PIONEER, two other early literary period-
> icals.

Studies of Individual Periodicals

THE ARGONAUT (1877-1907)

Arlt, Gustave O. "Bret Harte--the Argonaut." SOUTHERN CALIFORNIA
QUARTERLY, 44 (1962), 17-30.

Castro, Adolphe de. PORTRAIT OF AMBROSE BIERCE. New York: Century,
1929.

> Chapter V on "Bierce and Pixley" surveys the caustic relationship
> between the editor of THE ARGONAUT and the owner.

Hart, Jerome A. IN OUR SECOND CENTURY: FROM AN EDITOR'S NOTE-
BOOK. San Francisco: Pioneer Press, 1931.

> A former editor gives a thorough account of the periodical in chap-
> ters VIII through XI, "The 'Argonaut's' Beginnings," "Shop Talk,"
> "Early 'Argonaut' Contributors," and "A Roster of 'Argonaut'
> Writers." Hart's study places the magazine in the historical milieu
> of San Francisco in the last half of the nineteenth century.

McWilliams, Carey. AMBROSE BIERCE: A BIOGRAPHY. New York: Archon, 1967.

> Pp. 122-44 cover Bierce's association with THE ARGONAUT from its first issue on March 25, 1877, through his apparent editorship of the periodical, to his resignation from the staff in 1880. Bierce's editorial work from 1881 to 1886 on THE WASP, a satirical weekly, is investigated in Chapter IX.

O'Connor, Richard. AMBROSE BIERCE: A BIOGRAPHY. Boston: Little, Brown, 1967.

> Bierce's editorial work is discussed on pp. 108-19, with emphasis on the relationship he had with owner Colonel Frank Pixley, a relationship not helped by the difference of opinion as to "whether the ARGONAUT should be a literary journal (Bierce's concept) or a vehicle for anti-Irish invective (Pixley's)." Bierce's editorship of THE WASP is covered on pp. 135-48.

Wotherspoon, James R. "The San Francisco ARGONAUT, 1877-1907." Dissertation, University of California (Berkeley), 1962.

*　*　*　*　*

THE BASIS (1895-1896)

Keller, Dean H. "Albion W. Tourgee as Editor of THE BASIS." NIAGARA FRONTIER, 12 (1965), 24-28.

> Although THE BASIS contained mostly articles on politics and history, a significant amount of fiction and poetry did appear in it, much of it by the editor and his daughter, Aimee Tourgee. The magazine was published in Buffalo.

*　*　*　*　*

THE CHAP-BOOK (1894-1898)

Calkins, Earnest Elmo. "THE CHAP-BOOK." COLOPHON, Part 10. April 1932.

> Calkins views the periodical's format and artistry from a printer's point of view.

Katz, Joseph. "Stephen Crane to the CHAP-BOOK: Two New Letters." STEPHEN CRANE NEWSLETTER, 2 (Winter 1967), 9-10.

> Letters indicate that Crane submitted material to THE CHAP-BOOK as early as 1894.

Kramer, Sidney. A HISTORY OF STONE & KIMBALL AND HERBERT S. STONE & CO. WITH A BIBLIOGRAPHY OF THEIR PUBLICATIONS, 1893-1905. Chicago: Norman W. Forgue, 1940.

> "The CHAP-BOOK and Its Contemporaries," pp. 25-55, looks at

the magazine in the context of the 1890's literary scene with its phenomenal rise of little magazines, among them THE LARK, the PHILISTINE, and M'LLE NEW YORK.

* * * * *

THE DIAL (Chicago) (1880-1929)

"The DIAL, 1880-1900." THE DIAL, 28 (1900), 327-28.

This commemorative article briefly surveys THE DIAL's first twenty years of publication.

Mosher, Frederic J. "Chicago's 'Saving Remnant': Francis Fisher Browne, William Morton Payne, and THE DIAL (1880-1892)." Dissertation, University of Illinois, 1950.

Mosher investigates the literary and social ideas of editor Browne and his associates as reflected in THE DIAL and attempts to find the key to the journal's success during its first twelve years.

"The New DIAL." THE DIAL, 13 (1892), 127-28.

Reasons are given here for the magazine's change from a monthly to a semi-monthly, and plans for a changed format are announced.

"Supplement." THE DIAL, 13 (1892).

Articles on THE DIAL's early years are included here.

* * * * *

THE DIAL (Cincinnati) (1860)

Conway, Moncure Daniel. AUTOBIOGRAPHY, MEMORIES AND EXPERIENCES OF MONCURE DANIEL CONWAY. 2 vols. Boston: Houghton, Mifflin, 1904.

Pp. 306-16 of Volume I cover the author's editorship of THE DIAL.

* * * * *

THE GOLDEN ERA (1852-1893)

Mobley, Lawrence E. "Mark Twain and the GOLDEN ERA." PAPERS OF THE BIBLIOGRAPHICAL SOCIETY OF AMERICA, 58 (1964), 8-23.

Mobley lists Twain's contributions to THE GOLDEN ERA up to April 17, 1868, and then examines the writer's relationship to the magazine.

_____. "San Francisco's GOLDEN ERA: 1852 to 1860; Its Contents and Significance Plus Representative Selections and an Index of Contributors." Dissertation, Michigan State University, 1961.

Mobley examines the contents of this weekly literary journal founded in 1852 by two former gold miners. Although sentimentality had overcome the ERA's fiction by 1860, in the early years it promoted local-color literature that looked forward to the writings of Bret Harte and Mark Twain.

Taylor, Archer. "Biblical Conundrums in the GOLDEN ERA." CALIFORNIA FOLKLORE QUARTERLY, 5 (1946), 273-76.

Taylor lists forty-four conundrums found in THE GOLDEN ERA.

* * * * *

THE HESPERIAN (1838-1839)

Venable, W.H. "A Pioneer Author to a Pioneer Editor." OHIO ARCHAEO-LOGICAL AND HISTORICAL QUARTERLY, 1 (1887), 255-56.

A letter written in 1839 by author John McDonald to William D. Gallagher, editor of THE HESPERIAN, is reprinted here in full. McDonald expresses appreciation for a favorable review of his SKETCHES.

* * * * *

THE ILLINOIS MONTHLY MAGAZINE (1830-1832), later THE WESTERN MONTHLY MAGAZINE (1833-1837)

Shultz, Esther. "James Hall in Vandalia." JOURNAL OF THE ILLINOIS STATE HISTORICAL SOCIETY, 23 (1930), 92-112.

While in Vandalia, Hall founded THE ILLINOIS MONTHLY and edited it from 1830 to 1832.

* * * * *

THE LAKESIDE MONTHLY MAGAZINE (1871-1874), originally called THE WESTERN MONTHLY MAGAZINE (1869-1870)

"The Life-Story of a Magazine." THE DIAL, 54 (1913), 489-92.

This article on THE LAKESIDE MONTHLY had been written in 1874 for SCRIBNER'S MONTHLY, which at that time was about to absorb the Chicago periodical. However, when the agreement was broken the piece was never published. It traces the struggles of editor Francis Fisher Browne to make the LAKESIDE succeed in the face of numerous economic crises and the indifference of the Chicago public.

* * * * *

THE MIDLAND MONTHLY (1894-1899)

Wright, Luella M. "The Midland Monthly." IOWA JOURNAL OF HISTORY

AND POLITICS, 45 (1947), 3-61.

The first Iowa literary magazine is discussed in detail.

* * * * *

THE OREGON MONTHLY MAGAZINE (1852)

Nelson, Herbert B. THE LITERARY IMPULSE IN PIONEER OREGON. Corvallis, Oreg.: Oregon State College Press, 1948.

On pp. 68-69 Nelson discusses and reprints poems from the first magazine published on the Pacific Coast, THE OREGON MONTHLY MAGAZINE, AN ENTERTAINING MISCELLANY, DEVOTED TO USEFUL KNOWLEDGE AND GENERAL INFORMATION.

* * * * *

THE OVERLAND MONTHLY (1868-1875, 1883-1935)

Brady, Duer Somes. "A New Look at Bret Harte and THE OVERLAND MONTHLY." Dissertation, University of Arkansas, 1962.

Brady examines the MONTHLY's finances, contents, and editorial policies during Harte's editorship from July 1868 to December 1870.

Bridge, James Howard. MILLIONAIRES AND GRUB STREET: COMRADES AND CONTACTS IN THE LAST HALF CENTURY. New York: Brentano's, 1931.

On pp. 191-217 Bridge relates his experiences while editor of THE OVERLAND MONTHLY in the 1890's, including his association with Jack London during the writer's early career.

Harte, Bret. "General Introduction." THE WRITINGS OF BRET HARTE. Boston: Houghton, Mifflin, 1899. I, xi-xix.

The author recalls the publishing of "The Luck of Roaring Camp" in the second issue of THE OVERLAND MONTHLY. Both the printer and publisher of the magazine objected to the story on moral grounds.

_____. THE LETTERS OF BRET HARTE. Ed. Geoffrey Bret Harte. Boston: Houghton, Mifflin, 1926.

This collection includes letters written while Harte was editor of the OVERLAND (pp. 4-8).

James, George Wharton. "The Founding of the OVERLAND MONTHLY." THE OVERLAND MONTHLY, 52 (1908), 3-12.

A survey of the periodical's historical milieu precedes a discussion of its founding and an investigation of the contents of the first two issues.

May, Ernest R. "Bret Harte and the OVERLAND MONTHLY." AMERICAN

LITERATURE, 22 (1950), 260-71.

> May discusses the mutually-beneficial relationship of Harte and THE OVERLAND MONTHLY.

Merwin, Henry Childs. THE LIFE OF BRET HARTE, WITH SOME ACCOUNT OF THE CALIFORNIA PIONEERS. Boston: Houghton, Mifflin, 1911.

> Harte was the journal's first editor when it was founded in 1868, and his "The Luck of Roaring Camp," published in the OVERLAND after editorial debate, helped to establish his national reputation.

O'Connor, Richard. BRET HARTE: A BIOGRAPHY. Boston: Little, Brown, 1966.

> Pp. 97-132 examine the OVERLAND's history and Bret Harte's association with the periodical until he went East in 1871. One of the facts revealed is that Harte as editor and contributor did not always promote the West uncritically, as the magazine's owner would have preferred. O'Connor also discusses a fateful misunderstanding which prevented Harte from becoming editor of the Chicago LAKESIDE MONTHLY in 1871.

Pemberton, T. Edgar. THE LIFE OF BRET HARTE. New York: Dodd, Mead, 1903.

> Harte's editorship of the OVERLAND is covered on pp. 82-93, with emphasis on Harte's own literary development during the period and the publication's stormy relationship with the San Francisco public.

Skelley, Grant Teasdale. "The OVERLAND MONTHLY Under Milicent Washburn Shinn, 1883-1894: A Study in Regional Publishing." Dissertation, University of California (Berkeley), 1968.

> The OVERLAND was revived eight years after publication had ceased in 1875, and Skelley investigates this phase of its history.

Smith, Goldie Capers. "THE OVERLAND MONTHLY: Landmark in American Literature." NEW MEXICO QUARTERLY, 33 (1963), 333-40.

> This is a survey of "The OVERLAND MONTHLY: Landmark in American

Stewart, George R., Jr. BRET HARTE: ARGONAUT AND EXILE. 1931; rpt. Port Washington, N.Y.: Kennikat Press, 1959.

> Chapters XX, XXI, and XXII cover the founding of the OVERLAND by Anton Roman, his signing of Harte as the magazine's editor, and the friendships and experiences Harte encountered during his tenure in that position.

*   *   *   *   *

THE ROLLING STONE (1894-1895)

Barban, Arnold M. "The Discovery of an O. Henry ROLLING STONE." AMERICAN LITERATURE, 31 (1959), 340-41.

> "The April 21 [1895] ROLLING STONE is similar to other extant

issues of the paper, containing short stories, local-interest sketches, poems, jokes, humorous editorial comments, and some advertisements."

Ratchford, Fanny E. "The ROLLING STONE: the Life History of an O. Henry Rarity." COLOPHON, Part 17. June 1934.

O. Henry's humorous journal, called the ICONOCLAST for the first two issues, started in Austin, Texas, in 1894 and lasted one year. Ratchford discusses circulation, dates, and other publishing information.

*   *   *   *   *

THE SEMI-COLON (1845)

Tucker, Louis L. "The Semi-Colon Club of Cincinnati." OHIO HISTORY, 73 (1964), 13-26.

This literary society of the 1830's and 1840's published the short-lived SEMI-COLON magazine. The history and literary importance of the club are examined here.

*   *   *   *   *

THE THUNDERBOLT (1871)

Murphy, Lawrence R. "THE THUNDERBOLT: Primitive Literature from a New Mexico Mining Camp." NEW MEXICO QUARTERLY, 36 (1966), 175-80.

Murphy reprints "An Antediluvian Story," the "only memorable literary contribution" to the humorous magazine which appeared only three times in 1871.

*   *   *   *   *

THE WEEKLY OCCIDENTAL (1864)

Rogers, Franklin R. "Washoe's First Literary Journal." CALIFORNIA HISTORICAL QUARTERLY, 36 (1957), 365-70.

THE WEEKLY OCCIDENTAL, Nevada Territory's first literary periodical, lasted for only four issues in March 1864, and no known issues exist today.

*   *   *   *   *

THE WESTERN MESSENGER (1835-1841)

Blackburn, Charles E. "Some New Light on the WESTERN MESSENGER." AMERICAN LITERATURE, 26 (1954), 320-36.

Blackburn presents facts concerning the MESSENGER'S publishing history not given in previous investigations of the periodical.

Bolster, Arthur S., Jr. JAMES FREEMAN CLARKE: DISCIPLE TO ADVANC-
ING TRUTH. Boston: Beacon Press, 1954.

> Pp. 98-118 cover Clarke's editorship of the MESSENGER from 1836
> until 1839. He turned increasingly to England and New England
> instead of the local area for the magazine's literature.

Gohdes, Clarence. "THE WESTERN MESSENGER and THE DIAL." STUDIES
IN PHILOLOGY, 26 (1929), 67-84.

> The policies and contents of THE WESTERN MESSENGER, an early
> Transcendental periodical, anticipate those of THE DIAL. This
> article contains basically the same information as the chapter of
> the same title in Gohdes' THE PERIODICALS OF AMERICAN
> TRANSCENDENTALISM.

Scott, Leonora Cranch. THE LIFE AND LETTERS OF CHRISTOPHER PEARSE
CRANCH. Boston: Houghton, Mifflin, 1917.

> Cranch temporarily edited the MESSENGER during the absence of
> James Freeman Clarke (pp. 36-39). The book also contains two
> caricatures of THE DIAL group which appeared in the MESSENGER.

Thomas, John Wesley. JAMES FREEMAN CLARKE: APOSTLE OF GERMAN
CULTURE TO AMERICA. Boston: John W. Luce, 1949.

> The chapter entitled "Wanderjahre" (pp. 54-81) covers Clarke's
> editorial work on the MESSENGER from 1835 to 1840, focusing on
> his promotion of German literature and culture through his own
> contributions and his encouragement of others.

_____. "The WESTERN MESSENGER and German Culture." AMERICAN-GER-
MAN REVIEW, 11 (October 1944), 17-18.

> Through the pages of the MESSENGER middlewestern readers were
> introduced to German theological, philosophical, and literary ideas.

*   *   *   *   *

THE WESTERN MONTHLY REVIEW (1827-1830)

Folsom, James K. TIMOTHY FLINT. New York: Twayne, 1965.

> The third part of Chapter II (pp. 61-73) covers Flint's founding
> and editing of THE WESTERN MONTHLY REVIEW in Cincinnati.
> He wrote three-fourths of the material himself, mostly fictional,
> and his work is examined here.

Chapter 7

BIBLIOGRAPHIES AND CHECKLISTS

Chapter 7

BIBLIOGRAPHIES AND CHECKLISTS

General

Aderman, Ralph M. "James Kirke Paulding's Contributions to American Magazines." STUDIES IN BIBLIOGRAPHY, 17 (1964), 141-51.

> Paulding contributed to periodicals frequently throughout his career.

Barnes, Jack C. "A Bibliography of Wordsworth in American Periodicals Through 1825." PAPERS OF THE BIBLIOGRAPHICAL SOCIETY OF AMERICA, 52 (1958), 205-19.

> Included in this list are poems reprinted in American periodicals, reviews of Wordsworth, imitations and parodies, and articles that refer to the man or his work.

Beer, William. "Checklist of American Periodicals." PROCEEDINGS OF THE AMERICAN ANTIQUARIAN SOCIETY, 32 (1922), 330-45. This study was later published, New Orleans: Howard Memorial Library, 1924.

> Beer includes ninety-eight periodicals begun between 1741 and 1800. "The titles are given briefly, without bibliographical details of pagination and illustration, but the dates of beginning and conclusion, frequency of publication, size, place of imprint, and name of printer and publisher are given with exactness."

"Chapter XIX: Later Magazines." THE CAMBRIDGE HISTORY OF AMERICAN LITERATURE. Ed. William Peterfield Trent, et al. New York: G.P. Putnam's Sons, 1921. IV, 774-79.

> This is a bibliographical listing of books, chapters, articles, indexes, and checklists relating to literary periodicals in general and major ones specifically.

"Chapter XX: Magazines and Annuals." THE CAMBRIDGE HISTORY OF AMERICAN LITERATURE. Ed. William Peterfield Trent, et al. New York: G.P. Putnam's Sons, 1918. II, 511-16.

This listing includes the same kind of information as the entry above for periodicals which were published before 1850.

Davis, Richard Beale. AMERICAN LITERATURE THROUGH BRYANT, 1585-1830. Goldentree Bibliographies in Language and Literature. New York: Appleton-Century-Crofts, 1969.

Pp. 9-11 list major "Periodicals and Newspapers" and "Commentaries on Periodicals and Newspapers."

Ditzion, Sidney. "The History of Periodical Literature in the United States: A Bibliography." BULLETIN OF BIBLIOGRAPHY, 15 (1935), 110, 124-33.

The focus here is on literary periodicals. "The bases of selection have been authority, scholarship, length, and importance as 'new' material."

Faxon, Frederick Winthrop. A CHECK-LIST OF AMERICAN AND ENGLISH PERIODICALS. Boston: Boston Book Co., 1908.

_____. EPHEMERAL BIBELOTS. Boston: Boston Book Co., 1903. This list was first published as "A Bibliography of Ephemeral Bibelots." BULLETIN OF BIBLIOGRAPHY, 1 (1897-1899), 21-23; 3 (1902-1904), 72-74, 92, 106-7, 124-26.

Faxon gives details on the little magazines that appeared during the 1890's.

Firkins, Oscar W. WILLIAM DEAN HOWELLS: A STUDY. Cambridge, Mass.: Harvard University Press, 1924.

The "Bibliography" on pp. 339-46 includes Howells' contributions to magazines, with the dates of publication.

Ford, Paul Leicester. CHECK-LIST OF AMERICAN MAGAZINES PRINTED IN THE EIGHTEENTH CENTURY. Brooklyn, N.Y.: Historical Printing Club, 1889. This list also appeared in LIBRARY JOURNAL, 14 (1889), 373-76.

Although magazines had yet to become specialized, for many of them literature was already a primary interest.

INDEX TO AMERICAN PERIODICAL LITERATURE 1728-1870. New York: Pamphlet Distributing Co., 1941.

Part I, "The List of Periodicals Indexed," includes 339 journals. The following four parts list material found in these periodicals on "Edgar Allan Poe," "Walt Whitman 1819-1892," Ralph Waldo Emerson, and French fiction.

Jaffe, Adrian H. BIBLIOGRAPHY OF FRENCH LITERATURE IN AMERICAN MAGAZINES IN THE EIGHTEENTH CENTURY. East Lansing: Michigan State

College Press, 1951.

Joyce, Hewette Elwell. "Mrs. Browning's Contributions to American Periodicals." MODERN LANGUAGE NOTES, 35 (1920), 402-5.

> This annotated list includes poems contributed directly to American periodicals and not reprinted from other sources.

Lewis, Benjamin M. A GUIDE TO ENGRAVINGS IN AMERICAN MAGAZINES, 1741-1810. New York: New York Public Library, 1959.

> More than 650 engravings which appeared in fifty-nine magazines are listed. The three parts of this study list the engravings first according to the individual magazines in which they appeared, then by subject and title, and finally by engraver.

_____. "A History and Bibliography of American Magazines, 1800-1810." Dissertation, University of Michigan, 1956.

> Although this bibliography lists periodicals of all kinds, the most numerous are the literary miscellanies which published fiction, poetry, and especially serial essays, most of which were copied from English periodicals. The study includes a long historical introduction.

_____. "Preparing a Guide to Engravings in American Magazines: 1741-1810." BULLETIN OF THE NEW YORK PUBLIC LIBRARY, 63 (1959), 189-90.

_____. "Preparing a Register of Editors, Printers, and Publishers of American Magazines, 1741-1810." BULLETIN OF THE NEW YORK PUBLIC LIBRARY, 61 (1957), 517-21.

_____. A REGISTER OF EDITORS, PRINTERS, AND PUBLISHERS OF AMERICAN MAGAZINES, 1741-1810. New York: New York Public Library, 1957.

> Lewis has attempted to list every individual engaged in these activities during the period.

Middleton, Rev. Thomas C. "A List of Catholic and Semi-Catholic Periodicals Published in the United States From the Earliest Date Down to the Close of the Year 1892." RECORDS OF THE AMERICAN CATHOLIC HISTORICAL SOCIETY OF PHILADELPHIA, 4 (1893), 213-42. See also in the same publication Middleton's "Catholic Periodicals Published in the United States, From the Earliest in 1809 to the Close of the Year 1892: A Paper Supplementary to the List Published in These Records in 1893." 19 (1908), 18-41.

> Literary journals included in this list are so labelled.

Northup, Clark Sutherland. "Periodicals." A REGISTER OF BIBLIOGRAPHIES OF THE ENGLISH LANGUAGE AND LITERATURE. New York: Hafner Publishing Co., 1962. Pp. 273-86.

> This is a list of bibliographies and checklists, many of them, how-
> ever, for newspapers only. Pp. 278-82 specifically focus on Ameri-
> can periodicals and newspapers.

Rede, Kenneth, and Charles F. Heartman. "A Census of First Editions and
Source Materials By or Relating to Edgar Allan Poe in American Public and
Private Collections: Periodicals Contributed to by Edgar Allan Poe." AMERI-
CAN BOOK COLLECTOR, 2 (1932), 28-32, 141-53.

> Poe contributed to fifty-two known periodicals, and some of them
> are listed here, with short discussions of their editors and publishing
> history.

Schilling, Hanna-Beate. "The Role of the Brothers Schlegel in American Literary Criticism as Found in Selected Periodicals, 1812-1833: A Critical Bibliography." AMERICAN LITERATURE, 43 (1971), 563-79.

> Articles found in thirty-nine selected periodicals which discuss the
> Schlegels are listed and discussed. This study is intended to correct
> some of William Charvat's views in THE ORIGINS OF AMERICAN
> CRITICAL THOUGHT: 1810-1835.

Stephens, Ethel. AMERICAN POPULAR MAGAZINES: A BIBLIOGRAPHY. Boston: Boston Book Co., 1916.

> Items under such headings as "Scope and Influence" could be useful
> in a study of literary periodicals.

Tucker, Ethelyn D.M. "List of Books First Published in Periodicals." BULLETIN
OF BIBLIOGRAPHY, 1 (1897-1899), 11-12, 24-27, 41-43, 60-61, 77-79, 94-
95, 108-10, 124-26, 141-42, 154-55.

> Books are listed alphabetically according to author, and the volumes
> of the publications in which the serials appear are noted also.

New England

Matthews, Albert. LISTS OF NEW ENGLAND MAGAZINES, 1743-1800. Cam-
bridge, Mass.: J. Wilson & Co., 1912. This study first appeared as "New
England Magazines of the Eighteenth Century." PUBLICATIONS OF THE CO-
LONIAL SOCIETY OF MASSACHUSETTS, 13 (1910), 69-74.

> This unannotated list is organized according to year of publication.

RESEARCH KEYS TO THE AMERICAN RENAISSANCE: SCARCE INDEXES OF
THE CHRISTIAN EXAMINER, THE NORTH AMERICAN REVIEW, AND THE NEW
JERUSALEM MAGAZINE FOR STUDENTS OF AMERICAN LITERATURE, CUL-
TURE HISTORY, AND NEW ENGLAND TRANSCENDENTALISM. Ed. Kenneth

Walter Cameron. Hartford: Transcendental Books, 1967. This is a reprint in one volume of the following: Cushing, William. INDEX TO THE CHRISTIAN EXAMINER, VOLUMES I-LXXXVII, 1824-1869. Boston: J.S. Cushing, 1879; Cushing, William. INDEX TO THE NORTH AMERICAN REVIEW, VOLUMES I-CXXV, 1815-1877. Cambridge, Mass: John Wilson and Son, 1878; Wright, H.W. "Index to the NEW JERUSALEM MAGAZINE, Volumes I to XLIV." NEW JERUSALEM MAGAZINE, 44 (1872), 162-297. These indexes were also reprinted in AMERICAN TRANSCENDENTAL QUARTERLY, 4 (1969).

> THE NEW JERUSALEM MAGAZINE is a Swedenborgian journal subscribed to by Emerson and containing poetry.

The South

Atchison, Ray M. "Southern Literary Periodicals, 1732-1967." A BIBLIOGRAPHICAL GUIDE TO THE STUDY OF SOUTHERN LITERATURE. Ed. Louis D. Rubin, Jr. Baton Rouge: Louisiana State University Press, 1969. Pp. 82-89.

> This is a list of secondary sources relating to the periodicals.

Ellison, Rhoda Coleman. "Periodicals." A CHECK LIST OF ALABAMA IMPRINTS 1807-1870. University, Ala.: University of Alabama Press, 1946. Pp. 23-26.

> Descriptive annotations are included.

Gilmer, Gertrude. CHECKLIST OF SOUTHERN PERIODICALS TO 1881. Boston: F.W. Faxon, 1934.

> This checklist contains information on 757 periodicals of all kinds, including location, periodicity, and changes in title. In her "Introduction" Gilmer discusses "essay-periodicals" and "essay-journal-magazines," and talks about the heavy literary borrowing and short careers of southern magazines.

_____. "Maryland Magazines--Ante Bellum, 1793 to 1861." MARYLAND HISTORICAL MAGAZINE, 29 (1934), 120-31.

> Many of the periodicals listed here are literary publications.

Griffin, Max L. "A Bibliography of New Orleans Magazines." LOUISIANA HISTORICAL QUARTERLY, 18 (1935), 493-556.

> This annotated bibliography of "only those magazines that are of some literary significance and interest" includes a "Chronological Check-List" from 1834 to 1930 and an "Index of Editors and Principal Contributors."

Harwell, Richard Barksdale. CONFEDERATE BELLES-LETTRES: A BIBLIOGRAPHY AND A FINDING LIST OF THE FICTION, POETRY, DRAMA, SONG-

STERS, AND MISCELLANEOUS LITERATURE PUBLISHED IN THE CONFEDERATE
STATES OF AMERICA. Hattiesburg, Miss.: Book Farm, 1941.

> "Magazines and Newspapers," including a few literary periodicals,
> are listed on pp. 78-79. The introductory essay discusses a num-
> ber of southern literary journals.

Hoole, William Stanley. A CHECK-LIST AND FINDING-LIST OF CHARLESTON
PERIODICALS, 1732-1864. Durham, N.C.: Duke University Press, 1936.

> This list includes many literary journals and briefly describes the
> contents and aims of some of them.

The West

Dickey, Imogene B. "The Names and Editors of Early Texas Literary Magazines." OF EDSELS AND MARAUDERS. Ed. Fred Tarpley and Ann Moseley.
Commerce, Tex.: Names Institute Press, 1971.

Holland, Dorothy G. "An Annotated Checklist of Magazines Published in St.
Louis before 1900." WASHINGTON UNIVERSITY LIBRARIES STUDIES, 2 (1951),
1-53.

Lutrell, Estelle. NEWSPAPERS AND PERIODICALS OF ARIZONA, 1859-1911.
Tucson: University of Arizona Press, 1950.

> Although the introduction to this study discusses newspapers only,
> the bibliography lists some periodicals, and the annotations note
> such things as changes in title and editorship.

Scott, Franklin William. NEWSPAPERS AND PERIODICALS OF ILLINOIS,
1814-1879. Springfield: Illinois State Historical Library, 1910.

> This bibliography includes useful and detailed annotations. Although
> the "Introduction" focuses on newspapers, it does discuss THE ILLI-
> NOIS MONTHLY MAGAZINE, a frontier literary journal edited
> by James Hall in Vandalia in the 1830's (see Chapter VI).

Venable, W.H. "Literary Periodicals of the Ohio Valley." OHIO ARCHAEO-
LOGICAL AND HISTORICAL QUARTERLY, 1 (1887), 201-5.

> This is a list of "between sixty and seventy titles of periodicals
> devoted wholly or in part to general literature, that have appeared
> in the Ohio valley from the year 1819 to 1860...." A revised
> form of this list appears in Venable's BEGINNINGS OF LITERARY
> CULTURE IN THE OHIO VALLEY (see Chapter VI). Both lists in-
> clude dates, locations, and editors.

Chapter 8

BACKGROUND STUDIES

Chapter 8

BACKGROUND STUDIES

Beard, Charles A. and Mary R. THE RISE OF AMERICAN CIVILIZATION. 2 vols. New York: Macmillan, 1927.

> This cultural history mentions early literary periodicals on pp. 498-503 of Volume I, and the rise of the cheap magazines on pp. 465-67 of Volume II.

Boynton, Percy H. LITERATURE AND AMERICAN LIFE: FOR STUDENTS OF AMERICAN LITERATURE. Boston: Ginn, 1936.

> Boynton provides background material on various literary groups and sections of the country.

Branch, E. Douglas. THE SENTIMENTAL YEARS, 1836-1860. New York: D. Appleton-Century, 1934.

> Branch describes the cultural milieu of the period when GODEY'S LADY'S BOOK became firmly established and journals of high quality such as GRAHAM'S survived by including fashion plates and sentimental fiction.

Brooks, Van Wyck. MAKERS AND FINDERS: A HISTORY OF THE WRITER IN AMERICA, 1800-1915. 5 vols. New York: E.P. Dutton, 1952.

> The five studies included in this series are THE WORLD OF WASH-INGTON IRVING, THE FLOWERING OF NEW ENGLAND, THE TIMES OF MELVILLE AND WHITMAN, NEW ENGLAND: INDIAN SUMMER, and THE CONFIDENT YEARS. All are useful for background information on the social and cultural life of the nineteenth century.

Calverton, V.F. THE LIBERATION OF AMERICAN LITERATURE. New York: Charles Scribner's Sons, 1932.

> Calverton argues that a "colonial complex" and the petty bourgeois Puritan value system tyrannized American literature until the twentieth century. Such established journals as SCRIBNER'S MONTHLY,

HARPER'S MONTHLY, and THE NORTH AMERICAN REVIEW per-
petuated the conservative tradition until challenged by modern
periodicals such as POETRY and the NEW MASSES. Other nineteenth-century journals are also mentioned in the course of Calverton's discussion of this struggle for liberation.

Charvat, William. THE PROFESSION OF AUTHORSHIP IN AMERICA, 1800-
1870. Ed. Matthew J. Bruccoli. Columbus: Ohio State University Press,
1968.

These essays offer a useful background on the economics of publishing. Chapter IV on "Poe: Journalism and the Theory of Poetry"
discusses two obsessions in Poe's late years, the idea presented in
EUREKA and "a determination to establish what he envisioned as
the ideal monthly magazine," the PENN or STYLUS.

Clark, Harry Hayden, ed. TRANSITIONS IN AMERICAN LITERARY HISTORY.
Durham, N.C.: Duke University Press, 1953.

These essays trace the history of American literary thought from "The
Decline of Puritanism" to "The Rise of Realism, 1871-1891."

Commager, Henry Steele. THE AMERICAN MIND: AN INTERPRETATION OF
AMERICAN THOUGHT AND CHARACTER SINCE THE 1880's. New Haven:
Yale University Press, 1950.

The literary culture of the last years of the nineteenth century is
covered in the first chapters, and pp. 74-81 discuss the periodical
field.

Goddard, Harold Clarke. STUDIES IN NEW ENGLAND TRANSCENDENTAL-
ISM. New York: Hillary House, 1960.

This study of various aspects of Transcendentalism can serve as an
introduction to the philosophical basis for THE DIAL, THE WESTERN
MESSENGER, AESTHETIC PAPERS, and other literary journals.

Griswold, Rufus Wilmot. THE PROSE WRITERS OF AMERICA. 2nd ed. Philadelphia: Porter & Coates, 1870.

Griswold includes a long footnote in his first chapter (pp. 38-40)
evaluating a number of literary journals. Among figures discussed
in the book are editors Joseph Dennie and Robert Walsh.

Harte, James D. THE OXFORD COMPANION TO AMERICAN LITERATURE.
4th ed. New York: Oxford University Press, 1965.

This basic reference work includes entries on literary periodicals.

Horton, Rod W., and Herbert W. Edwards. BACKGROUNDS OF AMERICAN
LITERARY THOUGHT. 2nd ed. New York: Appleton-Century-Crofts, 1967.

"The purpose of this book is to provide in compact and relatively
simplified form certain historical and intellectual materials necessary to a fuller understanding of the leading American authors."

Howard, Leon. LITERATURE AND THE AMERICAN TRADITION. Garden City,
N.Y.: Doubleday, 1960.

Howard attempts "to seek out those attitudes of mind which controlled the creative imagination and helped shape the country's
literature toward a recognizable national character."

Jensen, Merrill, ed. REGIONALISM IN AMERICA. Madison: University of
Wisconsin Press, 1951.

The attitudes and cultures of various regions are investigated in
these essays. Benjamin T. Spencer's "Regionalism in American
Literature" (pp. 219-60) touches on the regional characteristics
and opinions of a number of nineteenth-century literary journals.

Kindilien, Carlin T. AMERICAN POETRY IN THE EIGHTEEN NINETIES. Providence, R.I.: Brown University Press, 1956.

Chapter I, "The Literary Scene," presents a background discussion
of the decade, and one passage discusses literary periodicals and
little magazines in their contemporary milieu.

Knight, Grant C. AMERICAN LITERATURE AND CULTURE. New York: Ray
Long and Richard R. Smith, 1932.

This study is divided into three parts: the literatures of "Coloniza-
tion," "Romanticism," and "Realism." Each part contains a brief
general discussion of the era's "Newspapers and Magazines."

_____. THE CRITICAL PERIOD IN AMERICAN LITERATURE. Chapel Hill:
University of North Carolina Press, 1951.

Knight states that his "intention in this book is to explain why the
battle between American romancers and realists reached a crisis in
the 1890's..." His discussion touches on magazines involved in
the debate.

Leisy, Ernest Erwin. AMERICAN LITERATURE: AN INTERPRETIVE SURVEY.
New York: Thomas Y. Crowell, 1929.

This survey doesn't specifically discuss periodicals, but "Appendix
B" briefly surveys periodical literature.

Mott, Frank Luther. GOLDEN MULTITUDES: THE STORY OF BEST SELLERS
IN THE UNITED STATES. New York: Macmillan, 1947.

Mott offers a background on the literary tastes of the American public.

Nye, Russel Blaine. THE CULTURAL LIFE OF THE NEW NATION: 1776-1830. New York: Harper & Row, 1960.

> Included in this cultural history is a chapter on "The Quest for a National Literature," a movement which involved a number of early literary periodicals, some of which are discussed.

Parrington, Vernon Louis. MAIN CURRENTS IN AMERICAN THOUGHT: AN INTERPRETATION OF AMERICAN LITERATURE FROM THE BEGINNINGS TO 1920. 3 vols. in 1. New York: Harcourt, Brace, 1958.

> Parrington's is one of the most thorough of American literary histories.

Pattee, Fred Lewis. THE FEMININE FIFTIES. 1940; rpt. Port Washington, N.Y.: Kennikat Press, 1966.

> Pattee examines the culture of the decade, and major and minor writers in relation to that culture. Chapter XXI, "Boston Builds a Magazine," covers the decline of Philadelphia as the center for literary periodicals and the founding of the ATLANTIC, the influence of which helped to counteract the sentimentality which had been dominant.

_____. THE FIRST CENTURY OF AMERICAN LITERATURE, 1770-1870. 2nd ed. New York: Cooper Square Publishers, 1966.

> Periodicals are discussed in Chapter XII, "Rise of the Reviews," covering THE MONTHLY ANTHOLOGY and the founding of THE NORTH AMERICAN REVIEW; Chapter XXXI, "The Magazinists," on journals of the period of GODEY'S and THE NEW YORK MIRROR; and Chapter XXXVI, "The ATLANTIC MONTHLY."

_____. THE NEW AMERICAN LITERATURE, 1890-1930. New York: Century Co., 1930.

> The first chapters of this book present a literary study of the 1890's. Chapter I, "The Fin De Siecle," specifically touches on the little magazine phenomenon and the resentment it stirred among literary conservatives.

Pritchard, John Paul. CRITICISM IN AMERICA: AN ACCOUNT OF THE DEVELOPMENT OF CRITICAL TECHNIQUES FROM THE EARLY PERIOD OF THE REPUBLIC TO THE MIDDLE YEARS OF THE TWENTIETH CENTURY. Norman: University of Oklahoma Press, 1956.

> A significant amount of criticism appeared in the journals, and Pritchard touches on some of these in the course of his investigation.

_____. LITERARY WISE MEN OF GOTHAM: CRITICISM IN NEW YORK, 1815-1860. Baton Rouge: Louisiana State University Press, 1963.

> Pritchard's study reveals much about the contents and policies of the

New York magazines in which the criticism is found. A section on "The Publication of Criticism in New York" (pp. 144-48) is especially informative on periodicals.

Quinn, Arthur Hobson, ed. THE LITERATURE OF THE AMERICAN PEOPLE: AN HISTORICAL AND CRITICAL SURVEY. New York: Appleton-Century-Crofts, 1951.

This detailed history includes discussions of Poe and Lowell as editors, and a chapter on the later nineteenth century as "The Age of the Monthly Magazine" (pp. 569-97).

Richardson, Lyon N. A HISTORY OF EARLY AMERICAN MAGAZINES, 1741-1789. New York: Thomas Nelson and Sons, 1931.

Although none of the magazines selected by Richardson for his study are literary, he goes into detail on their contents, economic problems, and rivalries to an extent that makes his work valuable as background to a study of literary periodicals.

Spiller, Robert E., et al., eds. LITERARY HISTORY OF THE UNITED STATES. 3rd ed., rev. New York: Macmillan, 1963.

This is the most basic and thorough of American literary histories.

Stovall, Floyd, ed. THE DEVELOPMENT OF AMERICAN LITERARY CRITICISM. Chapel Hill, N.C.: University of North Carolina Press, 1955.

Essays especially useful to anyone studying the literary journal are Richard H. Fogle's "Organic Form in American Criticism: 1840-1870" and Robert P. Falk's "The Literary Criticism of the Genteel Decades: 1870-1900." Fogle discusses critical views found in THE DIAL.

Taylor, Walter Fuller. A HISTORY OF AMERICAN LETTERS. Boston: American Book Co., 1936.

This is a good source for information on the works and ideas of a number of men of letters associated with literary journals.

Trent, William Peterfield, et al., eds. THE CAMBRIDGE HISTORY OF AMERICAN LITERATURE. 3 vols. in 1. New York: Macmillan, 1944.

Individual chapters on literary periodicals are listed in the second section of this study, "General Studies and Contemporary Views."

Wendell, Barrett. A LITERARY HISTORY OF AMERICA. New York: Charles Scribner's Sons, 1920.

Wendell first examines New England literary culture, and then the New York culture which he feels supplanted it. He glances at some literary periodicals in the course of his study and includes a chapter on 'Atlantic Monthly'" (pp. 370-77).

Wish, Harvey. SOCIETY AND THOUGHT IN MODERN AMERICA. 2nd ed. 2 vols. New York: David McKay, 1962.

This study offers a thorough background on the social and intellectual milieu in which literary journals were published.

Appendix A

LITERARY MATERIAL

IN NON-LITERARY PERIODICALS

Appendix A

LITERARY MATERIAL
IN NON-LITERARY PERIODICALS

THE ARENA (1889-1909)

Cline, H.F. "Benjamin Orange Flower and the ARENA, 1889-1909." JOUR-NALISM QUARTERLY, 17 (1940), 139-50, 171.

> Editor Flower's policies and the history of THE ARENA are covered here. The editor maintained high prestige for his journal while advocating radical reform.

_____. "Flower and the ARENA: Purpose and Content." JOURNALISM QUARTERLY, 17 (1940), 247-57.

> Flower's editing practices and the contents of THE ARENA are dis-cussed.

Dickason, David H. "Benjamin Orange Flower, Patron of the Realists." AM-ERICAN LITERATURE, 14 (1942), 148-56.

> Although he has been ignored or else disparaged by literary his-torians, Flower's interest as editor of THE ARENA in art for the sake of social reform was an important impetus for the rise of real-istic literature.

_____. "The Contribution of Benjamin Orange Flower and the ARENA to Critical Thought in America." Dissertation, Ohio State University, 1940.

Fairfield, Roy P. "Benjamin Orange Flower: Father of the Muckrakers." AM-ERICAN LITERATURE, 22 (1950), 272-82.

> Fairfield examines Flower's role as a reformer while editor of THE ARENA.

Reuben, Paul Purushottam. "Dynamics of New England Transcendentalism in Benjamin Orange Flower's ARENA (1889-1909)." Dissertation, Bowling Green State University, 1970.

> Flower was interested in Transcendentalism during a period when the movement supposedly had died out.

_____. "Thoreau in B.O. Flower's ARENA." THOREAU SOCIETY BULLETIN, 117 (1971), 5-6.

Flower recognized Thoreau's greatness long before most critics did.

_____. "Whitman in B.O. Flower's ARENA." WALT WHITMAN REVIEW, 19 (1973), 11-19.

Although he emphasized Whitman's views on religious freedom and equality at the expense of literary criticism, Flower deserves praise "for accepting studies of a literary rebel whose reputation even after his death was suspect."

Stallings, Frank Loyd. "Benjamin Orange Flower and THE ARENA: Literature as an Agent of Social Protest and Reform." Dissertation, University of Texas, 1961.

THE ARENA focused on political and social reform. Literature, however, was an important interest to editor Flower, and his literary opinions are examined here along with the social views that influenced them.

*   *   *   *   *

DEBOW'S REVIEW (1846-1880)

McMillen, James A. THE STORY OF DEBOW'S REVIEW. Baton Rouge: Otto Claitor, 1936.

This pamphlet sketches the REVIEW's history.

_____. THE WORKS OF JAMES D.B. DEBOW. A BIBLIOGRAPHY OF DE-BOW'S REVIEW WITH A CHECK LIST OF HIS MISCELLANEOUS WRITINGS IN-CLUDING CONTRIBUTIONS TO PERIODICALS AND A LIST OF REFERENCES RELATING TO JAMES D.B. DEBOW. Hattiesburg, Miss.: Book Farm, 1940.

This study includes a thorough bibliographical investigation of the REVIEW's history, and an examination of DeBow's editing of and contributions to other periodicals. The more literary of these journals were THE SOUTHERN QUARTERLY REVIEW and DEBOW'S WEEKLY PRESS.

Nachman, Selma. "A Collation of DEBOW'S REVIEW, Giving the Date, the Numbering, and the Title of Each Issue and Volume, From 1846 to 1880." BULLETIN OF THE BIBLIOGRAPHICAL SOCIETY OF AMERICA, 4 (1912), 27-32.

Nixon, Herman Clarence. "DeBow's Review." SEWANEE REVIEW, 39 (1931), 54-61.

Nixon examines DeBow's views on such issues as slavery and industrialization in the issues published during the fifteen years before the Civil War, and finds interesting contrasts with the views expressed in the magazine after the war from 1866 to 1870.

Skipper, Ottis Clark. J.D.B. DEBOW: MAGAZINIST OF THE OLD SOUTH. Athens: University of Georgia Press, 1958.

> DeBow's career, including his editorial activities before he launched DEBOW'S REVIEW, is covered in detail in this study. The RE-VIEW's policies and contents during various phases of its history are covered in chapters such as "Launching the REVIEW," "The RE-VIEW and Its Problems," "The REVIEW in Its Prime," and "The RE-VIEW After the War."

_____. "J.D.B. DeBow, the Man." JOURNAL OF SOUTHERN HISTORY, 10 (1944), 404-23.

> The REVIEW was the culmination of DeBow's strong desire to found and edit his own journal, and Skipper concludes that he was the best magazinist in the South. His earlier editorship of THE SOUTH-ERN QUARTERLY REVIEW is also covered here.

Standard, Diffee William. "DEBOW'S REVIEW, 1846-1880: A Magazine of Southern Opinion." Dissertation, University of North Carolina (Chapel Hill), 1970.

> The publishing history of the magazine and the views of the editor are examined.

*   *   *   *   *

THE FORUM (1886-1907)

Olsen, Norman laCour, Jr. "The FORUM as a Magazine of Literary Comment: 1886-1907." Dissertation, Duke University, 1963.

> Following an introductory history of the periodical, Olsen discusses THE FORUM's literary ideas.

*   *   *   *   *

THE INDEPENDENT (1848-1928)

Gladish, Robert W. "Mrs. Browning's Contributions to the New York INDEPEN-DENT." BULLETIN OF THE NEW YORK PUBLIC LIBRARY, 71 (1967), 47-54.

> In 1860 and 1861 Mrs. Browning published thirteen poems in THE INDEPENDENT. This article investigates her, and consequently Robert Browning's, contacts with this religious weekly and with its editor Theodore Tilton.

*   *   *   *   *

THE MARYLAND GAZETTE (1727-current)

Howard, Martha C. "THE MARYLAND GAZETTE: An American Imitation of the TATLER and the SPECTATOR." MARYLAND HISTORICAL MAGAZINE, 29 (1934), 295-98.

The literary contents of this weekly news periodical closely imitate the form and conventions of the Addisonian essay.

* * * * * *

THE NATION (1865-current)

Armstrong, William M. "The Writings of E.L. Godkin: An Essay and a Bibliography."" BULLETIN OF THE NEW YORK PUBLIC LIBRARY, 72 (1968), 288-327.

> The essay sketches Godkin's entire career, including his early associations with THE KNICKERBOCKER and THE NORTH AMERICAN REVIEW before his editorship of THE NATION.

McCormick, Edgar L. "Thomas Wentworth Higginson, Poetry Critic for the NATION, 1877-1903." SERIF, 2 (September 1965), 15-20.

> Higginson's views of contemporary poetry belie the conventional opinion that he is "simply a representative of the genteel tradition at its worst." Included here is an "Index to American Authors Given Especial Notice by Thomas Wentworth Higginson in 'Recent Poetry, NATION, 1877-1903."

Page, Evelyn. "'The Man Around the Corner': An Episode in the Career of Henry Adams." NEW ENGLAND QUARTERLY, 23 (1950), 401-3.

> In August 1879 THE NATION carried an anonymous unfavorable review of Adams' LIFE OF ALBERT GALLATIN, and editor Godkin was curious about the author's personal feelings about the review and reviewer. Adams was unaware that the critic was his brother, Charles Francis, Jr.

Sterne, Richard C. "Political, Social, and Literary Criticism in the New York NATION, 1865-1881: A Study in Change of Mood." Dissertation, Harvard University, 1957.

Van Doren, Carl. "Books and THE NATION," THE NATION, 121 (1925), 11-12.

> A former editor of the periodical praises the high quality of THE NATION's criticism and book reviews.

* * * * * *

THE NEW ENGLAND WEEKLY REVIEW (1828-1831?)

Currier, Thomas Franklin. "Whittier and the NEW ENGLAND WEEKLY REVIEW." NEW ENGLAND QUARTERLY, 6 (1933), 589-97.

> John Greenleaf Whittier edited THE NEW ENGLAND WEEKLY REVIEW in 1830 and 1831, and most issues of this predominantly political journal contained either a poem or prose piece by him during his tenure.

Appendix B

POE AND THE AMERICAN

LITERARY PERIODICAL

Appendix B

POE AND THE AMERICAN LITERARY PERIODICAL

Allen, Michael. POE AND THE BRITISH MAGAZINE TRADITION. New York: Oxford University Press, 1969.

> Trained in the British magazine tradition, especially represented by BLACKWOOD'S, Poe as editor attempted to strike a balance, however precarious, between an appeal on one hand to the intellectual few and on the other hand to the mass audience that made solvency for periodicals possible. Thus, while Poe despised the "namby-pamby" character of GODEY'S LADY'S BOOK and GRAHAM'S, he also lacked faith in periodicals like the DEMOCRATIC REVIEW and THE AMERICAN REVIEW because of their economic precariousness.

Boynton, Percy H. "Poe and Journalism." ENGLISH JOURNAL, 21 (1932), 345-52.

> Poe's literary achievement is placed in its journalistic context.

Campbell, Killis. "Poe and the 'Southern Literary Messenger' in 1837." THE NATION, 89 (1909), 9-10.

> Campbell attempts to ascertain Poe's activities in Richmond or on the MESSENGER throughout 1837, a year for which Woodberry in his biography (see below) could find less information than for any other.

Gill, William Fearing. LIFE OF EDGAR ALLAN POE. 4th ed. New York: W.J. Widdleton, 1877.

> This early biography covers Poe's work on THE SOUTHERN LITERARY MESSENGER, THE NEW YORK QUARTERLY REVIEW, BURTON'S GENTLEMAN'S MAGAZINE, GRAHAM'S MAGAZINE, THE SATURDAY MUSEUM, and finally THE BROADWAY JOURNAL.

Green, A. Wigfall. "The Weekly Magazine and Poe." ENGLISH STUDIES IN HONOR OF JAMES SOUTHALL WILSON. Charlottesville: University of Virginia Press, 1951. Pp. 53-65.

Poe's relationships with various periodicals are discussed.

Harrison, James A. LIFE OF EDGAR ALLAN POE. New York: Thomas Y. Crowell, 1903. This biography was also included in Volume I of THE COMPLETE WORKS OF EDGAR ALLAN POE. New York: Thomas Y. Crowell, 1902.

> Chapters VII, VIII, and X cover Poe's editorial activities on BURTON'S, GRAHAM'S, and THE BROADWAY JOURNAL. A "Bibliography of the Writings of Edgar Allan Poe" (pp. 431-55) lists contributions to various literary journals.

Hull, William Doyle. "A Canon of the Critical Works of Edgar Allan Poe with a Study of Poe as Editor and Reviewer." Dissertation, University of Virginia, 1941.

Ingram, John H. EDGAR ALLAN POE: HIS LIFE, LETTERS, AND OPINIONS. 1880; rpt. New York: AMS Press, 1965.

> Poe's editorial associations with various periodicals are discussed in this early biography, with an especially detailed examination of his work for GRAHAM'S in chapters XII and XIII, "Editor of GRAHAM'S MAGAZINE" and "Reverses."

Jackson, David K. POE AND THE SOUTHERN LITERARY MESSENGER. 1934; rpt. New York: Haskell House, 1970.

> Jackson examines Poe's work as editor and contributor to the MESSENGER early in his journalistic career, and considers this experience to be influential on Poe's later activities. Appendices are included that contain letters of MESSENGER publisher T.W. White to Lucian Minor and Beverley Tucker and a list of Poe's contributions to the periodical from 1835 to 1837.

_____. "Poe's Notes: 'Pinakidia' and 'Some Ancient Greek Authors.'" AMERICAN LITERATURE, 5 (1933), 258-67.

> Twenty-eight paragraphs, or fillers, which appeared in the MESSENGER are here attributed to editor Poe, and Poe's own sources for them are given when these can be determined. Jackson maintains that Poe's "Pinakidia," whose paragraphs are very similar to these MESSENGER items, was originally intended to be used as filler material in the magazine.

Jacobs, Robert D. POE: JOURNALIST & CRITIC. Baton Rouge: Louisiana State University Press, 1969.

> Jacobs feels that Poe's critical ideas must be viewed in the context of the journalistic pressures in which they were written in order to be clearly understood. He examines the criticism chronologically and in light of Poe's work as a contributor and editor of first THE

SOUTHERN LITERARY MESSENGER, and then the GENTLEMAN'S MAGAZINE, GRAHAM'S, and THE BROADWAY JOURNAL.

Kogan, Bernard. "Poe, the 'Penn', and the 'Stylus.'" THE SOUTHERN LITERARY MESSENGER, 2 (1940), 442-45.

If Poe had succeeded in his dream of establishing a literary periodical, he probably would have advanced the quality of such magazines in America generally.

Moss, Sidney P. "Poe and His Nemesis--Lewis Gaylord Clark." AMERICAN LITERATURE, 28 (1956), 30-49.

This examination of the Poe-Clark feud gives information on THE KNICKERBOCKER, Clark's journal, as well as GRAHAM'S and other periodicals with which Poe was associated.

_____. POE'S LITERARY BATTLES: THE CRITIC IN THE CONTEXT OF HIS LITERARY MILIEU. Durham, N.C.: Duke University Press, 1963.

Moss takes a position similar to Jacobs'--that Poe's critical ideas cannot be properly understood when isolated from the journalistic context in which they were expressed. This study examines in detail a number of the periodicals involved in Poe's campaign to break the stranglehold of the literary clique that he felt was stifling American literature.

Parks, Edd Winfield. EDGAR ALLAN POE AS LITERARY CRITIC. Athens, Ga.: University of Georgia Press, 1964.

Parks asserts that "Edgar Allan Poe was the first important critic to develop and to refine his critical theories through the media of book reviews and magazine articles." Consequently, in discussing Poe's critical ideas, Parks observes him closely as an editor of and contributor to various periodicals, and also looks at Poe's plans for the abortive PENN and STYLUS magazines.

Phillips, Mary E. EDGAR ALLAN POE THE MAN. 2 vols. Philadelphia: John C. Winston, 1926.

This biography includes useful details on Poe's work as an editor. It includes reprints in full of letters between Poe and Richard Burton, owner of the GENTLEMAN'S MAGAZINE, both at the time of Poe's initial appointment as editor and later when disagreements arose between the two men.

Poe, Edgar Allan. "The Literary Life of Thingum Bob, Esq." THE COMPLETE WORKS OF EDGAR ALLAN POE. Ed. James A. Harrison. New York: Thomas Y. Crowell, 1902. V, 1-27.

Poe satirizes editors of literary periodicals in this bogus biography.

_____. "Peter Snook." THE COMPLETE WORKS OF EDGAR ALLAN POE. Ed. James A. Harrison. New York: Thomas Y. Crowell, 1902. XIV, 73-89.

>After discussing an example of English periodical literature, the author concludes that most of the literature appearing in American periodicals is of inferior quality.

_____. "Some Secrets of the Magazine Prison House." THE COMPLETE WORKS OF EDGAR ALLAN POE. Ed. James A. Harrison. New York: Thomas Y. Crowell, 1902. XIV, 160-63.

>Poe attacks the chronic pirating of English literature by American magazine editors. However, he notes that the ones who do pay for American contributions should send the money to the financially needy writers more quickly than they do.

Pollin, Burton R. "Poe's Iron Pen." DISCOVERIES IN POE. Notre Dame, Ind.: University of Notre Dame Press, 1970. Pp. 206-29.

>Pollin discusses Poe's attempts to establish his own magazine, the STYLUS or PENN.

Quinn, Arthur Hobson. EDGAR ALLAN POE: A CRITICAL BIOGRAPHY. New York: D. Appleton-Century, 1941.

>Quinn gives a thorough account of Poe's work on the periodicals, including specific material such as Poe's letters to Lowell about THE PIONEER. Appendix IX lists "Contracts for the 'Broadway Journal.'"

Rede, Kenneth, and Charles F. Heartman. "A Census of First Editions and Source Materials By or Relating to Edgar Allan Poe in American Public and Private Collections: Periodicals Edited by Poe." AMERICAN BOOK COLLECTOR, 1 (1932), 274-77.

>Poe's editing of the following journals is discussed: THE SOUTHERN LITERARY MESSENGER, THE GENTLEMAN'S MAGAZINE, GRAHAM'S, THE NEW MIRROR, and THE BROADWAY JOURNAL.

Simpson, Lewis P. "'Touching "The Stylus"': Notes on Poe's Vision of Literary Order." STUDIES IN AMERICAN LITERATURE. Eds. Waldo McNeir and Leo B. Levy. Baton Rouge: Louisiana State University Press, 1960. Pp. 33-48.

>Simpson discusses Poe's attempts to found his STYLUS or PENN magazine and sees these attempts as reflections of Poe's desire to impose a critical order on the chaos of American letters.

Spivey, Herman E. "Poe and Lewis Gaylord Clark." PMLA, 54 (1939), 1124-32.

>The enmity between Poe and the editor of THE KNICKERBOCKER

began in 1843 when Clark rejected a Poe article on "Our Magazine Literature," later published in THE NEW WORLD. The feud
intensified as Clark attacked Poe through his magazine and Poe
responded in GRAHAM'S and GODEY'S.

Webb, Howard W., Jr. "Contributions to Poe's 'Penn Magazine.'" NOTES
AND QUERIES, 203 (1958), 447-48.

Poe collected a number of contributions for his projected magazine,
all of them falling short of his idealistic editorial goals.

White, William. "Edgar Allan Poe: Magazine Journalist." JOURNALISM
QUARTERLY, 38 (1961), 196-202.

This article surveys Poe's connections with various literary journals.

Woodberry, George E. THE LIFE OF EDGAR ALLAN POE. 2 vols. 1913;
rpt. New York: Biblo and Tannen, 1965.

Much of Poe's correspondence relating to literary periodicals is
revealed in this biography. For example, Woodberry publishes
letters which Poe wrote in his search for financial support for THE
BROADWAY JOURNAL.

INDEX

INDEX

Page references to sections on individual periodicals have been underlined.